THE SHARING OF THE GREEN

Other books by this author

A Pattern of Government Growth 1800–1860: The Passenger Acts and their Enforcement

Ireland: The Union and its Aftermath

Early Victorian Government 1830–1870

The Inspector General: Sir Jeremiah Fitzpatrick and Social Reform, 1783–1802

States of Mind: Two Centuries of Anglo-Irish Conflict, 1780–1980

The Hereditary Bondsman: Daniel O'Connell 1775–1829

The Emancipist: Daniel O'Connell 1830–1847

O'Connell

Jane Austen: Real and Imagined Worlds

The sharing of the green

A modern Irish history for Australians

Oliver MacDonagh

ALLEN & UNWIN

*For Catharine and Daniel, Emily
and Nicholas, Caitlin and Clare,
Alexander, Patrick and Hugo.*

First published 1996
Allen & Unwin Pty Ltd
9 Atchison Street, St Leonards, NSW 2065 Australia

National Library of Australia
Cataloguing-in-Publication entry:

MacDonagh, Oliver.
  The sharing of the green: a modern Irish history for
Australians.

  Includes index.
  ISBN 1 86373 911 4.

  1. Irish—Australia—History. 2. Ireland—History.
  3. Ireland—Politics and government. 4. Ireland—Social
conditions. I. Title.

941.5

Set in Garamond by DOCUPRO, NSW
Printed by Southwood Press, NSW
10 9 8 7 6 5 4 3 2 1

Contents

The provincial boundaries do not coincide with the political in the case of Ulster. Counties Donegal, Cavan and Monaghan are part of the Republic of Ireland.

Preface

This is not a book about the Irish in Australia but an attempt to describe the sort of world—or rather worlds, for they keep changing—from which the Irish came. It is a brief history of modern Ireland written with an Australian readership always in mind.

My notion of Irish history for Australians covers the period when Irish emigration to Australia was heaviest and the years that immediately followed the last major inflow. Practically, this meant a concentration on c.1790–c.1945 with an epilogue that sketches the main developments in Ireland over the past fifty years. The opening chapter tries to set out the case for the entire undertaking.

I have sought to stress those aspects and patterns of the modern Irish past that have had most bearing, as I see it, on the evolution of the Australian colonies, and later states and federation. This accounts for the emphasis on religion, land, protest, respectability, the role of the state, attitudes to authority, the imperial connection, separatism and above all politics, both organisational and aspirational.

Much of this is, of course, appropriate matter for any readership. But to some extent there are horses for courses. For example, I pay less attention in this book to health, capital, the Great Famine, international influences and similar distinctive factors than if it were an Irish history for Americans; less attention to Ulster Presbyterianism, planned settlement or the Atlantic trade than if it were an Irish history for Canadians; less attention to the Irish economy *per se* or language policy or art or literature than if it were a general Irish history.

The principle of selection has been the implications of one national history for another. This is not to suggest for a moment that Australian history should be regarded as derivative. National histories mesh (more or less, according to time, and place and circumstance) with other national histories. J.R. Seeley's famous description of history as a 'seamless web' may be by now a threadbare phrase; but still it describes the real indivisibility of historical forces, shuttling back and forth.

If we glance briefly at the Irish–Australian relationship from the Irish side, we can certainly say that nineteenth-century Irish history would have been very different without mass emigration to the areas hungry for white settlement, such as the Australian colonies. We can certainly say that the Parnellite and post-Parnellite Irish parties rested, in no small measure, on Australian resources. We can certainly say that the Australian model was of great significance in John Redmond's exposition of the Home Rule case in the first decade of the present century.

Even these few examples make the point that the influence of one country on another is not incompatible with but generates interaction.

On quite another tack, it is interesting to note the stability of the religious and ethnic composition of the white population of the Australian colonies throughout the nine-teenth century. This is in sharp contrast to the United Kingdom. When the constitutional union of Great Britain and Ireland took place in 1801, these proportions were much the same as those that were to prevail in Australia. But within half a century the United Kingdom had under-gone dramatic changes in both the distribution of population and the relative strength of the regional economies. Can the Australian experience open our eyes to the realised potentialities in the British–Irish relationship, had the proportions and relativities of 1801 stayed fixed? I do believe so.

Again, as Professor O'Farrell once wrote (of early nineteenth century Catholicism in Ireland and New South Wales), 'Ireland might learn much more from her colonies than she is currently wont: a simple one-way traffic of scholarship is inappropriate'. And indeed, where are Ulster historians now looking for an elucidation of the part played by the Battle of the Somme in 1916 in crystallising the Northern Protestant sense of identity and nationhood, but to the exemplar of Gallipoli and Australia in the preceding year.

Certain things lie out of reach. There are dimensions of the immigrants' experience which cannot be set down hard and fast. The Irish countryside, from which the great majority of the immigrants derived, may be described—though what a variety is encompassed in so small an island. The Irish climate, covering and feeding this landscape with cloud, mist, shower and intermittent sun, may be statistically rendered. But how did it feel to exchange such an encasement for an Australian physical environment which was in many places and at certain points the very opposite? When, and how completely, was the past overlaid and the new envelope of life become customary?

It is the same with time-scale, seasonality and all the other natural elements that surround and stamp childhood and adolescence. The immigrants had left a world where the traces or memorials of former centuries instilled a sense of age-old social processes, of a long tribal march, of which they were an essential item. How did it feel to be translated into an apparently bare landscape, with no understanding of the new land's immemorial meanings, invisible to the unseeing eye? How was it to know that 'home' was much too distant ever to be seen again, or that one now lived in an expanse into which more than half a hundred Irelands could be fitted, or to find that the hereditary rhythm of the seasons on which so many of the European patterns rested no longer formed the framework of the year?

These were all considerable matters for each first immigrant generation, with perhaps considerable effects upon Australia's future. But, by their very nature, they are not really measurable by the historian. The reader must do some of his or her own work and, from the known, infer and imagine something of the impalpable accompanying emotions. No less than Jane Austen herself once pleaded.

I do not write for such dull elves
As have not a great deal of ingenuity themselves.

I completed this work while a Professor at the Australian Catholic University and for its support I am most grateful. I owe very warm thanks to Mrs Pamela Crichton for her usual meticulous work on my behalf, to Miss Maureen O'Sullivan and Mrs Beverley Gallina for endless patience in dealing with my untidy drafts, to Dr Richard Reid for allowing me to draw on his great expertise for illustrations, to Professors Iain McCalman and John Ritchie for valued criticism and advice, and to my daughter, Melisa, for her encouragement when I was flagging. My gratitude to my wife grows all the more as my need for her support increases. As the nonagenarian congratulated on his long 'innings' said, 'The bowling gets better all the time'.

Oliver MacDonagh
May 1995

Introduction

Why Irish history for Australians? The first, most obvious and overwhelming answer is the quantitative. The 'average' Australian of today, if such a being there is, would be one-fifth Irish derived. In the racial pool of modern Australia, as calculated recently by Dr Charles Price, the Irish element is almost 20 per cent, exceeded only by the much larger English component, and well ahead of any other, even the Scots. Had a similar calculation been made in 1900, the Irish element would probably have exceeded one-quarter and might well have been almost one third. This represents a proportion of 'Irishness' considerably higher than anywhere else on earth, the homeland itself excepted. It is far larger than the American or any other equivalent.

Relative to the size of the host society, the Irish amounted to a prodigious Australian inflow. Irish visitors to Australia are often amazed to find, especially in country towns, the names on shopfronts mirroring those of Thurles or Ennis. Australian visitors to Ireland are often amazed at the number of familiar faces they see on Dublin's Grafton Street or along the Mardyke in Cork. The sheer original numbers are the reason why. They are also a prime reason for Australians to know something of modern Irish history if they are to comprehend the derivation of a large part of themselves.

Viewed against the vast Irish exodus of over eight million between 1788 and 1914, the number who emigrated to Australia, voluntarily or involuntarily, may seem in itself quite small. Although, for various reasons, it is impossible to be precise, the total was almost certainly between 400 000 and 500 000, about 50 000 of whom were convicts. However, the numbers were never small as a fraction of the white population of the day. At no stage in the nineteenth or early twentieth century did the Irish-born and those of principally Irish ancestry constitute less than 25 per cent of the whole body of white Australians, to say nothing of admixtures of Aboriginal and Irish blood. Even in the colonies (after 1901, states) where they were fewest, Tasmania and South Australia, they formed very considerable minorities. This meant that, unlike the Irish in most other places of settlement overseas, they were a founding and a forming people. Whatever the category, whether convicts, gaolers, soldiers, policemen, storekeepers, administrators or free settlers, they formed a large element in it from the very start. Rather than entering an allotted place in an already fixed and layered society, they played a significant part in the shaping of colonial institutions, attitudes, language and living patterns while these were still in their most fluid early stages.

This points to a second answer to the opening question: the timing of the Irish immigration or, more precisely, its steadiness and regularity. In most other countries in which Irish settled in great numbers, there were considerable variations in their volume of emigration from decade to decade, and even more in the proportion of the total immigration that this particular volume represented from time to time. For instance, the Irish and Germans dominated immigration into the United States in the later 1840s and early 1850s but were heavily outnumbered by other bodies of immigrants later in the nineteenth century. Of course, the fraction of Australian immigration that was Irish showed

The convict ship Lady Kennaway, *which left Cork on 27 October 1834 bound for Hobart. Approximately 45 000 (or 28 per cent) of the 160 000 convicts sent to Australia were Irish. (National Maritime Museum, Greenwich, negative no. A6406)*

some change season by season. But speaking generally it remained proportionate.

Not only were the Irish (almost uniquely in their case) a founding people in Australia, but also—despite occasional minor gaps and fluctuations—Irish immigration of 20–35 per cent was a constant throughout the most formative stages of Australian development after 1788. This meant a profound contribution to Australian culture, popular and political especially; to Australian social mores and habits; and to the Australian temperament and speech—for new societies are very plastic, and the first handling often sets the shape. In addition, the timing of their arrival meant that, geographically speaking at least, the Irish were distributed remarkably evenly across the colonies—remarkable, that is, when compared with their location in their other main areas of settlement. It was especially significant that they were proportionately numerous on the land. Such was not the case in any other region of the world, even if modern research suggests that they were more widely dispersed throughout the United States than the old stereotype of their ending up as essentially a 'Big City' people had implied.

Irish history provides the key to several of the major themes of Australian history. Let us take just one example here, religion. Sectarian division was almost as potent a factor as the divisions of race and class throughout the colonial period and for many years thereafter; and much of this had Irish roots. When we speak of the nineteenth century Irish, we are speaking of three main groups, generally, though not exclusively, to be distinguished by their religion. Roman Catholics constituted almost three-quarters of the home population, Anglicans (adherents of the Established Church or Church of Ireland) about 15 per cent and Presbyterians almost one in ten. Ultimately, the Irish in Australia reflected these proportions fairly faithfully, in every sense. It is important to stress this particular division because religion (or the religious tradition from which one derived, in the case of the indifferent or actual unbelievers) was perhaps the greatest of all dividers in the homeland.

Here again, the early date and the proportions of the Irish immigration are important. Between 1790 and 1830 Irish Protestants, the great majority of whom were at that stage Irish Anglicans, were well represented in the upper echelons of early colonial society. Traditionally, a high proportion of the younger sons and less well-connected members of the Irish Ascendancy had sought careers in the imperial or armed services which led them to spend long periods, and sometimes settle, overseas; and in post-1788 Australia this tradition continued to flourish. In their own fashion, however, Irish Catholics shared some of the benefits of participating in the first waves of European immigration. White Australia began late enough for a few professionally educated Catholics to be among its pioneers; and a small minority of Catholic convicts and poor Catholic immigrants were able enough, or lucky enough, to take advantage of the comparative fluidity of the class and economic structures at the time. In consequence, even in early nineteenth century Australia the Catholic Irish were to be found at almost all levels, although disproportionately many fewer the higher one ascended in the social scale, and disproportionately more numerous the lower one went down. To lump them together as a permanent and undifferentiated underclass would be quite misleading.

None the less, it was not without reason that they were commonly so regarded, and that they commonly regarded themselves in this way, at any rate before the First World War. Australia was dissimilar to other major areas of Irish overseas settlement, and in particular to the most important of these areas, the United States, in that no really large-scale immigration from elsewhere took place to push them upwards in the host society or to provide them with the chance to assume the leadership of the excluded and exploited. There was no Australian equivalent to the vast inflow of Italians, Scandinavians, Germans, Eastern Europeans or Russian and Polish Jews into the United States in the second half of the nineteenth century. Consequently, there were in Australia no new rungs added to the bottom of the social ladder whereby the Catholic Irish were, almost automatically, raised *en masse*. Nor was there any real equivalent to the post Civil War migration of blacks to the American north and mid-east, where colour prejudice, added to their other disadvantages, condemned them, in general, to the worst-paid and most despised forms of labour.

In these circumstances, it is easy to understand why the image of the Australian Catholic Irish remained so long that of the lower working class. The image matched the reality to a considerable extent. Yet it also masked the reality of Catholic upward social mobility even before 1914. Contrariwise, it has been apparent to all that, in the wake of the new post-1945 migrations, the Catholic Irish (that is, Irish by principal derivation) have tended to join the 'master races' in Australia. There are now few areas of power, riches or prestige in which they are under-represented. There are even some, such as politics and law, in which the opposite might well be the case.

During the nineteenth and early twentieth centuries, however, the Irish religious divisions deeply affected Australian political and social life, even to the third and fourth generations of immigrant stock. Various qualifications must be made to this generalisation. Some immigrants, of course, discarded religion altogether in their new home or were subsumed into other traditions. Nor was the correlation between religion and political stance always absolute; certain leading Irish Anglican immigrants of the early 1850s, for example, had been Young Irelanders. Again, there were at some stages significant political differences among even the Irish Catholic immigrants. In particular, the division between 'moral force' and 'physical force' Nationalists ran deep.

It must also be remembered that the degree of Irish communal distinctiveness, in action, depended on the Australian issue at stake. If the question were, say, one of opposition to Chinese settlement, the Catholic Irish were probably indistinguishable in their attitude from the great majority of their fellow white Australians. If the question were, say, which district should benefit from some particular public outlay, then the Catholic Irish voted with their neighbours rather than with their 'community' as such. If, however, the issue were denominational education, the Catholic Irish formed a virtually solid bloc and acted in concert to achieve their end.

In general, the Catholic Irish constituted the largest and most coherent minority group in the Australian colonies, as well as being peculiarly widely spread. One consequence of their numbers and dispersion was that they very rarely possessed sufficient political power in a constituency or ward to dominate it absolutely, but equally that they were rarely so few as to be insignificant as a local faction. This form of electoral and public influence might stand as a type or symbol of the general place and bearing of the Irish Catholics in pre-1914 Australian society as a whole.

The special parts played by Irish Anglicans and Irish Presbyterians and other nonconformists are also components of Australian colonial history. It is true that, taken as a whole, they were much closer in attitude and allegiance to, and far more easily assimilated by or with, their English and Scottish counterparts. But equally their Irish derivation and experience set them apart, to a significant extent, at any rate in the first and second generation. Irish history makes clear why this should have been so. Their society of origin was one in which sectional upbringing stamped outlooks and self-images very deeply.

A fourth response to the original question is that the Irish immigration was a peculiarly complex population movement, if only because Ireland itself was a deeply riven island. The religious divides alone affected—or were liable quickly to affect—almost every aspect of Irish life. Protestantism and Catholicism might be temporarily overlaid; but they were the ultimate magnetic poles for almost every phenomenon, social as well as political, in Ireland. The fact that Irish emigration to Australia reflected more or less the denominational proportions at home makes it all the more important to understand the respective derivations and peculiar cultural predispositions of each group.

Class, to take another instance, had a special complexity in Ireland. The great bulk of Irish immigrants were of rural origin; and the conventional categorisation of labourer, cottier (or renter of a small plot, year by year) and tenant farmer, particularly before 1850, suggests differences in economic and social status that scarcely existed in reality. Cottiers and labourers were often farmers' brothers, uncles, sons or nephews, for most tenant farmers down to the Great Famine rented ten acres (4 ha) or less. Conversely, in Ireland in the later nineteenth century entry into the professional classes was much more common, proportionately, than was the case in England, with corresponding differences in income, and propensity to emigrate. Similar examples of deviation from British social patterns can be readily found. To know who the Irish in Australia really were in their beginning, we must unpeel their layers and examine critically the conventional nomenclatures.

A final reason 'Why Irish history for Australians?' is that Ireland was subject to most extraordinary changes over the years 1780–1945. No European country had a more dynamic and disruptive experience, though doubtless it was equalled in other places. Despite the fundamental 'integrity of their ancient quarrels' (to use Churchill's phrase), each Irish generation was in a significantly different situation, with significantly different experiences, from its predecessor, and to comprehend fully the Irish impact here, we should certainly distinguish according to phase and epoch. For Irish influences in Australia were continual as well as continuous. Period by period, Irish emigration kept feeding Irish changes into the developing Australian systems, reflecting shifts in Irish fate or feeling, generation by generation. Hence the importance of following the flow of Irish history—or perhaps I should say its turbulent falls, slacks and races. The chapters that follow attempt to set out and explain the peculiarities of each little phase.

The conquest of Ireland begun by the Norman invasion of 1169 was not finally completed until the last remnants of native resistance were crushed at the Battle of Kinsale in 1601; even then it was again temporarily challenged, in the context of general European wars, in the 1640s and 1690s.

By the early eighteenth century, however, British control of Ireland was total and secure. The Irish Houses of Parliament acted as mere instruments of British policy. The Irish executive, centred around a Lord Lieutenant appointed by the British government, and operating from a single centre, Dublin Castle, carried out that policy practically unopposed. Local power rested with the Protestant Ascendancy, the descendants of the successive waves of planters of the sixteenth and seventeenth centuries, with their recruits from native ranks and their supporting bodies of middle- and lower-class Protestants—the Presbyterians and other dissenting sects, to some extent, excepted.

Despite some manifestation of opposition in the 1750s and 1760s, it was only on the eve of 1788 itself that this general state of things was at all seriously threatened.

1

Ireland in 1791

On 26 November 1791 the first convicts sent directly from Ireland reached Sydney Harbour. What of the country they had left behind?

Religious division

Every history is a tangle of threads. It is hard to know which best to pick in order to begin untangling. In the case of late eighteenth century Ireland, however, there is no need to hesitate for long. Religion was the most basic divider of society in almost all its aspects. The sectarian pattern had been set in the years immediately following the victory of William of Orange at the Battle of the Boyne in 1690. Woe to the vanquished. The Catholics, who had still held 60 per cent of Irish land only fifty years before, were now practically expelled from the rank of landowners. By confiscation and legal pressures to conform to Anglicanism, their holdings fell to less than 5 per cent of the land area of the island within two generations of the Williamite triumph; and land ownership was the essential source, and indicator, of wealth, social standing and political power during the eighteenth century.

Expropriation was the crux. The Catholics, three-quarters of the Irish population, were reduced, with comparatively few exceptions, to a servile status; and the Penal Laws (a succession of repressive statutes passed between 1691 and 1727) were set up to keep them permanently in that degraded state. One section of the laws militated against their possessing land, their status as gentry or gentlemen, and their membership of most of the professions or even crafts. Another section sought to ensure that they were denied education at home and forbidden to seek it abroad. A third was aimed at the eventual extinction of the Catholic religion. The presence of bishops and regular or 'order' priests in Ireland was prohibited and measures were enacted to guard against the existing parochial clergy being renewed. These decrees were supplemented by the establishment of various institutions to bring up Catholic orphans and unwanted children as Protestants.

Despite the third arm of the penal code, the effort to Protestantise the Irish masses was half-hearted and perhaps never seriously meant. It was convenient in many ways to have a helot base for the society. Correspondingly, persecution for religion's sake was only spasmodically undertaken even in the most dangerous years, 1715–45, when the restoration of the Catholic Stuarts to the British throne still seemed a real possibility. But the economic and social degradation of the Catholics of Ireland was resolutely pursued throughout the first half of the eighteenth century. This was the essential purpose of the laws. Protestant security was supposed to require absolute Protestant Ascendancy, which in turn necessitated a monopoly of every form of power—landed, legal, political and military. It was a form of colonial oppression and exploitation, though a curious form in that the subject people not only were indistinguishable in physical features from the masters but also were enabled (and in theory encouraged) to change castes by the simple device of abjuring one religion and conforming to another.

'Protestant' in this eighteenth century context meant Anglicans, members of the Established Church of Ireland. It did not include Presbyterians or any other nonconformists. Indeed, contemporaries always spoke of Protestants and Dissenters as separate bodies, resolutely maintaining the distinction between the Establishment Protestants and the rest instead of acknowledging the common cause of all those inimical to the Church of Rome. There was good reason for drawing this particular line. Irish nonconformists were also heavily discriminated against, even if their 'penal laws' fell far short of those arrayed against the Catholics. Because of their numbers, their geographical concentration in the north-east corner of the island and their unbending principles, the Presbyterians were singled out for extraordinarily harsh treatment by the Irish government. For most of the eighteenth century they were excluded not only from Parliament but also from all public offices and positions of honour or authority. Initially, even their education and public worship were restricted. Presbyterian clergy were persecuted for celebrating marriages; and the Church of Ireland declared that those so married were living in sin and their children illegitimate. Thus, it is far from a figure of speech to describe the eighteenth century Irish Presbyterians as second-class citizens. Their resentment of their debased condition ran correspondingly deep, and (unlike the Catholics) they displayed it freely.

By 1750 Ireland was well settled into a tri-sectored society. Well over four-fifths of the population, the Catholics and the Dissenters, were by reason of religion excluded from its government, and most of these—the great Catholic majority—were otherwise heavily oppressed. Even among the small Anglican minority in Ireland, only a comparative handful of great families enjoyed the fruits of exclusive privilege to the full. Many members of the Church of Ireland were middling or small farmers, tradesmen or shopkeepers, or even lower on the social scale, with little more than their sense of caste dominance and various occasional and occupational favours to reward them for their adherence to the official creed.

For several reasons, the penal code began to weaken in the latter half of the century. First, the Irish Catholics had proved quiet and loyal during the final Stuart bid to regain the British throne in 1745; moreover, a handful of them began to attain the respectability of wealth when, debarred by law from other occupations, they turned to, and made a success of, trade and money-dealing. Next, as the Enlightenment spread westwards from the Continent so too did religious toleration and the feeling that religion itself was a declining political force. Finally, the Williamite land resettlement, now unchallenged by the deprived for two generations, had come to seem increasingly secure, while more and more Catholics were conforming to the Established Church in order to gain or retain estates or to enter the main professions, especially law. In these circumstances, it seemed safe enough to relax a little the legal repressions of both Catholics and Dissenters, and by the end of the third quarter of the century concession had reached the stage of legislative reform. In 1772 the Irish Parliament made the first move towards allowing Catholics to lease land, and two years later it allowed them to attest their loyalty to the state by a declaration similar to one actually drawn up by a member of the Catholic episcopate. Shortly after, state employment was opened for Presbyterians by the repeal of the sacramental test by which they had hitherto been debarred from public office.

Spasmodic concessions continued in the 1780s, so much so that by 1791 a new crisis had been reached in religion in Ireland. The governing class was by now riven over whether to yield further to the Catholics or to call a halt. Gradually, apprehension of the social and political consequences of further relaxations had begun to permeate their ranks. A growing number of Irish Anglicans had come to regard their securities as threatened by the steady Catholic advance, and majorities in both Houses of the Irish

Parliament were resistant to further change. The Dissenters, and in particular their main component, the Presbyterians, were also divided on the issue. Despite their own recent 'liberation', more and more of them succumbed to their inherent distaste for popery. Many began to see the Catholics as deadly rivals for such economic and social advancement as they themselves had attained. This was especially the case where the population was religiously mixed and intense competition for tenancies had developed. In all sections of Irish Protestantism there were still considerable bodies who saw their own interests—to say nothing of their own general principles—as best served by an alliance with the Catholics. Catholic support, such people believed, was vital in any struggle for parliamentary reform or Irish legislative independence. But a polarisation of Protestant opinion had set in, and already the anti-Catholic pole was exercising the greater magnetism in even the most radical division of Irish Protestants, the Presbyterians.

There were now, however, two new forces in the field. The first was the British government, which was adopting more and more the role of the Catholics' friend. This was to be explained in part as an acknowledgment of the loyalty manifested by Catholics during and since the American War of Independence; in part, because the Revolution launched in France in 1789 made it incumbent to find support wherever possible, and the Catholic Church was a natural ally in the fight against irreligion; and in part to offset the over-mighty Irish Protestant Ascendancy by using the Irish Catholics as a counterweight. Moreover, the British, at a safe distance, could not truly empathise with the Irish Protestants' fears of eventual dispossession, and perhaps even annihilation. For all these reasons, they were pressing further moves towards Catholic Emancipation upon an increasingly reluctant Irish governing class. Second, the principal Catholic pressure group, the Catholic Committee, which had hitherto been dominated by members of the nobility and gentry, pursuing policies of obsequious request and discreet lobbying, was captured in 1791 by a radical group of merchants. Thereupon the aristocrats seceded. The new leaders began to press for full and immediate emancipation, as a matter of right instead of favour; and with the British government already much disposed to conciliate the Catholics, their cause did not seem hopeless.

Thus the religious issue was at a critical stage in 1791. On the side of further Catholic concession were ranged the respective Catholic leaderships (despite their tactical and social quarrels), the majority of the British Cabinet and their appointees in the Irish administration, the small minority of liberals and radicals among the Irish MPs and peers, and the rather larger minority of liberals and radicals among the northern Presbyterians. Against these stood the solid anti-Catholic majorities in both Irish Houses of Parliament, the bulk of the Irish Presbyterians and other Dissenters, and almost all the native—and by definition Anglican—members of the Irish government and judiciary. The heterogeneous parties seemed set on a collision course.

Political division

In 1791, as at all earlier junctures, the religious question was also a political question. It was closely interwoven with the most crucial element of politics, power—in both its narrowest and widest senses. Since the 1690s, ultimate power over Ireland had rested in London, with the English Parliament and government, at Westminster and Whitehall. But all residual power lay with the thin layer of major office holders, great landed proprietors, substantial gentry, higher clergy and judges who constituted the true Anglo-Irish Ascendancy. By *Poynings Act* (1494) the British Privy Council was enabled to regulate Irish legislation and by the *Declaratory Act* (1719) the British Parliament could even legislate directly for Ireland. But the day-to-day management of the Irish Parliament demanded some less severe mode of rule than a simple reliance on these ultimate sanctions.

For much of the eighteenth century, the British government maintained control of both Irish Houses by a system of local 'undertakers'. In effect, it farmed out the business of running the Irish Parliament to a few leading political magnates. In return it gave them a more or less free hand in emptying the cornucopia of Crown offices, sinecures, favours and money itself into the laps of their clients and supporters. Eventually, in the 1760s, an able Lord Lieutenant, Viscount Townshend, irritated by the extravagant demands and pretensions of the undertakers, brought them to heel by building up a Dublin Castle party, committed to following the British line of policy, in both Houses.

The American War changed the situation dramatically. In the place of the British troops removed from Ireland to fight in the North American theatre, Volunteer corps (in the end, some 100 000 strong) were formed for national defence. This created a powerful extra-parliamentary pressure group, many of whom were northern Presbyterians or middle or lower middle class members of the Church of Ireland. Comparatively speaking, it was a democratic force and developed certain comparatively democratic aims, some of them self-interested, some altruistic. At the same time, the Ascendancy was also involved, to a certain extent, in the new movement. They had old scores to pay off against their British overlords, as well as the desire to assert a *safe* degree of national, or at least parliamentary, independence. So long as the war lasted, the rise of this liberal spirit in Ireland, combined with Britain's temporary weakness, produced a succession of legislative reforms. During the years 1776–83, *Poynings Law* and the *Declaratory Act* of 1719 were repealed; Irish overseas trade was freed from British regulation; and appeals to the British House of Lords from Irish judicial decisions were disallowed.

Yet, when in 1783–84 the next stages in the process—reform of the Irish House of Commons and the admission of Catholics to fuller (if still far from full) citizenship—were proposed by the radicals who now dominated the Volunteer

7

movement, they were flatly rejected by the bulk of the Irish ruling class. It was, of course, this class that stood to lose much of its power and most of its electoral 'property' if the parliamentary seats it controlled were to be genuinely contested. Equally of course, the same class had been weakened *vis-à-vis* the British government once the American War ended, and Britain could once again devote serious attention and considerable resources to its Irish problem. But the most fundamental reason of all for calling a halt to the process of concession was fear that a liberated Catholic majority would ultimately tear down the entire edifice of Ascendancy. John Fitzgibbon, a lawyer of remarkably clear mind and utterance, put the point with stark simplicity when he told the gentlemen of Ireland that

> . . . the only security by which they hold their property, the only security which they have for the present establishment in church and state, is the connection of the Irish Crown with, and its dependence upon the Crown of England . . . if they are now duped into idle and fantastical speculations . . . under the specious pretence of asserting national dignity and independence, they will feel [the effects] to their sorrow[1].

To this unflattering assertion, that they were absolutely incapable of defending their own interests by themselves, the Ascendancy as a whole had to give a surly and reluctant assent.

On paper, Ireland had achieved in 1782 something approximating to what the twentieth century was to call 'dominion status'. On paper, its constitutional standing more or less matched that of post-Federation Australia. The reality was very different. The British government regained more or less effective control of the Irish Parliament soon after that body shied away from the further reform program. Even in terms of making real the formal 'independence' gained in 1782, the Patriots (as the Irish parliamentary opposition termed themselves) failed to capitalise on the opportunities offered them in the late 1780s. Their language might be aggressive, but their actions were very cautious. None the less, Anglo-Irish relations were now inherently unstable. Britain could not—or at any rate would not—depend forever on the purchase of votes and the playing on fears in both Irish Houses to counteract the Houses' undoubted constitutional right to pursue their own aims in everything from international commerce to the succession to the throne of Ireland, which was theoretically distinct from that of Britain. As early as the mid-1780s the Duke of Rutland, then Lord Lieutenant, predicted that, given the anomalous political situation, 'without *an union* Ireland will not be connected with Great Britain in twenty years longer'.[2]

By 1791 things had become still more critical. 'War changes everything', Thucydides wrote, and although war had not yet broken out between France and Britain, it was increasingly clear that the two were heading for armed conflict. One consequence was the granting in that year of various concessions to British, though not to Irish, Catholics; the continued opposition of the Irish Parliament to further Catholic reform seemed all the more grievous to its victims. A second factor was the great spur given to advanced liberals and radicals in Ireland by the overthrow of absolute monarchy and aristocratic domination in France. It was on the crest of this wave of feeling that the Catholic Committee again changed both its leadership and the range of its political demands. Equally significant was the formation late in 1791 of the Society of United Irishmen, at first in Belfast and then in Dublin. The guiding spirit in this development was an ardent young middle-class Protestant barrister, Theobald Wolfe Tone. Tone was neither the most original nor the most extreme of the founding group, but his was the most winning personality, the quickest mind and the readiest pen and tongue. Earlier in 1791 he had come to be employed as secretary (in effect, organisational manager) of the Catholic Committee, and crystallised his ideas in a critically important pamphlet, *An Argument on Behalf of the Catholics of Ireland*.

9

Tone had already come to the conclusion that British domination was the essential and inveterate source of Irish ills. The remedy (he argued) was Irish parliamentary reform because British power in Ireland was centred in its control of the Irish Parliament; and the critical step towards this reform was Catholic Emancipation so that the Irish people could present a united front to their oppressors, British and native alike. Tone was not yet a separatist: he still sought no more than equality and distinctiveness for Ireland within the Empire. Still less was he, as yet, committed to violence or even to considering seriously whether it might be necessary.

All the same, the identification of the Irish nation with the entire population of Ireland, and the demand for a thoroughly democratic parliamentary reform, and complete parity of civil rights and status for both Catholics and Dissenters, were revolutionary claims; and in the atmosphere of the 1790s they were all too likely—as indeed proved to be the case with Tone himself—to advance to calls for total separation from Great Britain and an ultimate resort to physical force.

In these ways also, 1791 saw decisive moves towards irrepressible and probably bloody conflict in Ireland. The United Irishmen were not yet a large body, but the Society concentrated and gave resolution to Irish middle (and a few upper) class radicals, especially among the Presbyterians of the north-east. It also tied them, in spirit, to the increasingly violent and uncompromising course of events in France. Meanwhile, partly owing to the link between the Society and the Catholic Committee provided by Tone, the advanced members of the Catholic mercantile class were being drawn into the campaign for drastic political change. Explosive materials of several sorts were being quickly assembled in Ireland in the year in which its first batch of convicts reached Australia. These convicts left Ireland too early to have been much influenced by the new revolutionary beliefs. But their immediate successors were to experience a rapid and violent upturning of many received ideas.

Secret societies

All this was confrontation above the surface. From the early 1760s onwards, confrontation of another sort had spread throughout the countryside and especially through east Munster and south Leinster. We may conveniently label this 'Whiteboyism', taking the name from the original movement of peasant protest. The Whiteboys represented the first concerted and powerful counter to the increasing burden of tithes (paid to the Protestant Church of Ireland), raised rents, enclosures and spreading pasturage that marked the mid-eighteenth century in Western Europe. Peasant counter-action was a common phenomenon at this time. But in no other place did it exhibit the regularity, persistence and comprehensiveness of Ireland. There (in contrast to England and Wales) labourers bore tithes, had no Poor Law to fall back on, and could hope for little town or industrial employment. Under pressure, and especially as population mounted, their condition grew proportionately more desperate.

Whiteboyism was distinguished by three special features: it was oath-bound and conspiratorial in form; it relied on mass support, or at least mass neutrality, and sought to use the pressure of numbers to secure its ends; and it aimed at stabilising various economic relationships within society. The first of these features led naturally to harsh internal and external discipline, and quasi-military forms. Whiteboy punishments of resisters and transgressors of their code were usually swift and cruel. Doubtless, they were also occasionally a cover for personal vengeance or extortion. We know comparatively little of the command structure of the Whiteboy movement, but this much at least is clear: that it involved a captaincy system, uniforms, martial display to intimidate others, the building up of arms and, at times, quite sophisticated planning.

Whiteboy violence and intimidation were directed quite as much at the enlistment or implication of large numbers in the movement as at direct and immediate objects. 'Swearing-in' of other peasants took place (under threat or persuasion) on isolated farms at night or on estates before the general expiration of leases or, most commonly perhaps, after Sunday mass, when all the parish was collected and particularly vulnerable to demands to constitute a common front. In 1786 in fact, one Catholic bishop tried to check the spread of conspiracy by closing all chapels and suspending mass in his diocese for a time. The wide enlargement of the agrarian secret societies had two purposes: first, to ensure a safe environment for the Whiteboy operations, and second to frighten the authorities into concession by the terrifying prospect of innumerable hordes ranged behind the demands.

Finally, although the movement grew out of particular tithe increases and enclosures of common land in Co. Tipperary, it soon developed, as it swept backwards and forwards across the country in later years, a very wide range of objectives. Together they fell little short of a coherent program. The regulation of rents, leases and tithes were the most common aims, but employment and wages, food and other prices, county tax, tolls, hearth money, and birth, marriage and death dues to the Catholic clergy were also areas of struggle. Thus, Whiteboyism constituted an effort, not to win political power or religious equality, but to deploy countervailing force for economic ends. These ends were conservative. Rents, tithes, dues, tolls, taxes and the rest were not attacked in themselves, but were accepted as elements in a received social order. It was innovation, arbitrariness and above all what seemed to be exorbitance that were resisted. It was the 'moral economy' of the rural masses, their conception of the right relations between

12

The Protestant Standard

"THIS IS THE SECRET OF ENGLAND'S GREATNESS." HOLY BIBLE "ENGLAND'S GLORY."

A JOURNAL OF POLITICAL AND RELIGIOUS FREEDOM.

NO. 14, VOL. I.   SATURDAY, JULY 31, 1869.   PRICE SIXPENCE.

The Protestant Standard

A JOURNAL OF POLITICAL AND
RELIGIOUS FREEDOM.

THE *Standard* will be published at the office, 377, Pitt Street, for the country post, and every Saturday morning, for the city. Agents will be supplied on Friday evenings. The *Standard* will advocate an enlightened and liberal policy in politics, and freedom from the trammels of Popery, the absurdities of Puseyism, and Ritualism, in Religion. In religious questions the principle of the Scriptures will be exclusively inculcated. Denominationalism will be carefully avoided. The object of the *Standard* will be to maintain and extend the principles of "our common Protestantism," that is, "our common Christianity," without favour to any of the Churches or sects into which the community is divided. The *Standard* belongs to no Church, unless to the church which is made up of all the Evangelical Churches. It will not depart from the broad platform of the Evangelical religion of the New Testament.

Terms of Subscription:

Yearly, payable in Advance	... ...	£1 0 0
Half-yearly, ditto	... ...	0 11 0
Quarterly, ditto	... ...	0 6 0
Single Copy ...	... ...	0 0 6

Subscribers in the country and distant parts must forward money either in Post Office Orders, in favour of Mr. SAMUEL GOOLD, or in Postage Stamps.

Terms for Advertisements:

Three lines, and under	... ...	£0 1 0
Eight ditto, ditto	... ...	0 2 0
Per one inch	... ...	0 2 0
Each successive inch	... ...	0 2 0

AGENTS AND CANVASSERS LIBERALLY DEALT WITH.

PROTESTANT Alliance Friendly Society.

Registered under the Friendly Societies' Act.

THE OBJECTS of the above Society are to relieve the Widows and Orphans of deceased members—to provide medicine and medical attendance—and, in case of sickness to make such allowance as is provided by the Rules of the Society.

Meetings held first Tuesday in the month in the Temperance Hall, Pitt Street.

Any information may be obtained from the following officers of the Society:—

JOHN DAVIES, Junr., President, 86, York st.
HUGH M'MILLAN, Vice-President, Sussex st.
JAMES GRAHAM, Secretary.
SAMUEL KIPPAX, Treasurer, New Mark George-street.

Ship Chandlery.

ON SALE by the undersigned—Europe' Coir-Manilla, and Wire Rope in all sizes, Stockholm Pitch and Tar, Oakum, Oars, Twine (all kinds) Canvas, Blocks, Paints, Anchors, Chains, Flags, Bunting, Metal, Copper and other Nails, China, Colza, Castor, Neatsfoot, and Black Oils, Turps, Kerosene, &c., &c.,

A. D. ARMSTRONG and CO.,
Market Wharf.

Artificial Teeth.

MR. J. SPENCER, Surgical and Mechanical Dentist, 352, George-street, over Mountcastle's. Received HONORABLE MENTION in Exhibition for Artificial Teeth. A single Tooth from 7s 6d. Teeth Scaled, Stopped, and Extracted. Children's teeth carefully regulated. Artificial Teeth re-modelled and repaired.

JOHN G. HANKS,
Wholesale and Retail Grocer,
529, GEORGE STREET,
and
NEWTOWN ROAD, SYDNEY.

JOHN DAVIES,
IRONMONGER AND GENERAL BLACKSMITH,
90, YORK STREET.

*** Smiths' work of every description. Railway Contractors' Tools of every description made on the most reasonable terms. Stoves repaired.

Loyal Orange Institution.

MEETINGS OF LODGES.

No. 1.

MEETS on the last WEDNESDAY in the month, at the Chapel, Kent-street, near King-street, at half-past Seven o'clock.
WILLIAM COULTER, W.M.
G. ACHESON, Secretary.

No. 2.

SCHOMBERG LODGE, meets on the second WEDNESDAY in the month, at the Chapel, Kent-street, at half-past 7 o'clock.
By order of W.M.
A. M. C. SCOTT, Secretary.

No. 4.

NO SURRENDER LODGE, Regular Monthly Meeting first WEDNESDAY, Chapel, Kent-street.
ROBT. McNEIL, Secretary.

No. 6.

GLADESVILLE meets in the Lodge Room, first MONDAY in the month.
By order of W.M.
SAMUEL JORDAN.

No. 7.

MEETS on the third TUESDAY in the month, at the Chapel, Kent-street, near King-street. Special Meetings convened by circular and advertisement.
A Grand Soiree and Musical and Literary Entertainment, in connection with the above, will be held in the Masonic Hall. For particulars see further advertisement.
By order of W.M.

No. 8.

PARRAMATTA meets in the Lodge Room the second THURSDAY in the month.
By order of
S. HART, W.M.
T. SHEPHERD, Sec.

No. 9.

MEETS on the second THURSDAY in the month at the Wesleyan School-room, Botany Road.

No. 10.

MEETS every first THURSDAY in the month, at the Chapel, Kent-street.
By order of W.M.
ALEX. McNEILLY, Sec.

No. 16.

REGULAR MONTHLY MEETING, second WEDNESDAY in each month.
By order of W.M.
THOMAS GRIFFITH, Sec.

No. 17.

VOLUNTEERS LOYAL ORANGE LODGE. The Members of the above Lodge hold their Regular Monthly Meeting on the third WEDNESDAY in each month at half-past 7 p.m., in the Chapel, Kent-street, near King-street.

No. 18.

THE "BOYNE" meets on the third MONDAY in the month, at Eight o'clock, in the Methodist Chapel, Myrtle-street, Darlington.

No. 22.

WYCLIFFE LODGE, meets in the Lodge-room, Kent-street, on the last MONDAY of each month.
J. KENNEDY, W.M.

Loyal Enniskillen Lodge, No. 25.

MEETS in the School-room, Chippendale, the first THURSDAY in the Month.
By order of the W.M.

No. 27.

ROYAL WILLIAM, Orange Lodge, meets second FRIDAY in each month, at the Lodge-room, Ebenezer School-room, Riley-street, at 7·30 p.m.
By order of W.M.
R. T. McNEILLY, Sec.

VOLUNTEER'S LOYAL ORANGE LODGE, No. 17.

THE ANNUAL SOIREE

will be held in the Temperance Hall, Pitt-street, on THURSDAY, August 12th. William Hewlett, Esq., J.P., in the chair. Tea on the table at 6·30 sharp. Tickets 2s. each. To be had at this Office, or from any member of the Committee.

No. 60.
Knights of Malta and Black Preceptory,
Under the Scotch Constitution.

MEETS on the Third MONDAY in the month, at half-past seven o'clock p.m., in the Chapel, Kent-stre t, near King-street.
By order of Sir E. K.C.
JAMES KAY, Secretary.

Sit hoc, hoc fidt.

Royal Chapter of Black Knights,
Encampment No. 146.
Under the Grand Black Chapter of Ireland.

MEETS at the Chapel, Kent-street, on the last Tuesday in each month, at 7·30 sharp. By order of the Right Worshipful Master, A.M.
A. M. C. SCOTT, Registrar, J.J.

New South Wales Protestant Political Association.

MEETINGS HELD AT THE ROOMS Kent-street, near King-street, every alternate Friday Evening, at 8 o'clock.
RICHARD McCOY, |
GEORGE BALMER, | Hon. Sec.

PROTESTANT POLITICAL ASSOCIATION.—South Sydney and Waterloo Branch.—Future Meetings will be called by a circular from the Branch Council.
H. T. TICKNER, Secretary.

JOSEPH WEARNE,
ANCHOR FLOUR MILLS,
FOOT OF
BATHURST STREET, SYDNEY.

Superfine Silk-dressed Flour, Seconds, Kiln-dried Corn Flour, &c., the best and cheapest in Sydney.

Pratt's Balsam of Horehound, for Coughs, Colds, and Influenza.

COPY of letter received from the Rev. J. D. THANE, late of Young, Lambing Flat.

Mr. W. PRATT

DEAR SIR.—The relation of the following fact as bearing testimony to the efficacy of your Balsam of Horehound, gives me pleasure. Whilst residing at Young, about a year ago, Mrs. P., a member of my congregation, had for some months been suffering from a most distressing cough, accompanied by spitting of blood, which all the ordinary means had failed to check. Thinking that some alleviation of her suffering might be afforded thereby I gave her one of the Bottles of your Balsam with which you kindly furnished me. The result so exceeded my expectation for in a few days not only did the expectoration cease, but a perfect cure was effected.

You are at liberty to use this letter as you please. I am, Dear Sir, yours faithfully, J. D. THANE, late minister of the Congregational Church at Young.
Sydney, March 6th, 1867.

Pratt's Balsam of Horehound.

Is prepared exclusively by W. PRATT, 521 George Street, Sydney Opposite Wiltshire Place.)

landlord and tenant, farmer and labourer, producer and consumer, that they sought to maintain or re-establish.

The Whiteboys were originally free from sectarianism. In fact, in the earliest years, Protestants were occasionally to be found as members. But as the movement crept northwards to Meath, Louth and the Ulster border counties in the 1780s, its character changed. It could be readily adapted to defending the particular economic interests of either the Protestants or the Catholics in places where Protestants were both numerous and poor, and saw their livelihoods endangered by a Catholic upsurge. Although it was the Catholics who appropriated the title 'Defenders'—and the Defenders did indeed act at times as a bulwark against physical and psychological assault—it was the Protestant Oakboys who really represented the defensive idea inherent in early Whiteboyism. As Catholics competed ever more effectively for leases and employment, Protestants saw the traditional order threatened by an increasing power from below.

The northern Protestant conspiracy, the Oakboys, was a repetition of the Munster Catholic one. It too sought the re-establishment of a 'moral economy' and by similar organisation, methods and forms of force. Much the same was true of the Orange Order that came into being in 1795. In many regards, the Orangemen were the natural successors of the Protestant Oakboys. Both bodies were frightened of social and economic dislocation, terrified by the prospect of being displaced by Catholics. It was the same sudden exorbitance and the same vision, or rather nightmare, of role reversal that brought both bodies into—and kept both in—being. We are, of course, familiar with their descendants, even to the present day.

By the 1790s the masses over much of the country had been habituated to extra-legal systems of regulation, enforced by secret associations and the threat of arms. Although the Whiteboys' objectives were not directly political in the conventional sense, their operations had instilled lessons in organisation, popular discipline and the

14

application of pressure that were to have a lasting effect on Irish politics. The subterranean agrarian movements formed the background to many things. First, they help to explain the viewpoint and conduct of the early Irish convicts in Australia, as well as, in a more general way, certain persistent Irish Australian attitudes towards party management and the land. Second, they laid the basis for popular agitation on an unprecedented scale and of an unprecedented compactness and flexibility. One of the crucial elements in the great Emancipation and Repeal campaigns of the early nineteenth century in Ireland was the obedient solidarity of huge numbers of directed people. Third, and more immediate, they also laid the basis for the violence that was to characterise the later 1790s, both by the precedents of armed action and by the accumulation, over many years, of arms hidden in peasant cottages and other caches. In addition, the bloody clashes of Catholic Defenders and Protestant Oakboys, and similar rural conspiracies on either side, prepared the way for the coming sectarian outbreaks. Fourth, Whiteboyism and its successors had important contributions to make to the Revolutionary movement of the near future. They provided organisational apparatus well-fitted for underground operations as well as the idea of alternative government from below, defying, and in a sense superseding, the official state.

It was never to be expected that the government would not respond violently to the challenge to its authority and the endangering of the interests of the ruling class. From the 1760s on there had been periodic mobilisations of state power to stamp out agrarian outrages and conspiracies. These reached a climax with the *Whiteboy Act* passed by the Irish Parliament in 1787. This severe measure gave the government wide powers to break up assemblies and otherwise use force to crush combinations; it also laid down ferocious punishments for administering or taking illegal oaths. In this way, the course of savage repression had been embarked on, and the machinery of savage repression set in place, well before Ireland was disturbed by the revolutionary events in France.

Thus in 1791 peasant politics, no less than grand and open politics, were approaching a crisis. The upheavals of that very year in rural France opened strange vistas, whether terrifying or exhilarating, to all classes in the local population.

Prosperity?

The last twenty years of the eighteenth century have gone down in popular tradition as a rare period of economic prosperity in Ireland. This is not altogether unwarranted, despite the fact that the tradition is partly attributable to a romanticisation of the years 1782–1800, the brief interval of Irish constitutional 'independence', and especially of its hero, the charismatic (but ultimately cautious) liberal orator, Henry Grattan, with whose name the little epoch has always been popularly identified. The keys to Ireland's relative years of plenty are, paradoxically, the onset of Britain's industrialisation and a more rapid increase in Ireland's population. Industrialisation turned Britain into a net corn importer. Indirectly, it helped to turn Irish agriculture to the growing of crops, and especially cereal production; a significant proportion of the produce was exported to the British market. The increase in the Irish population was closely linked to the more intensive farming. Why such an increase took place is a much debated and perhaps ultimately unanswerable question. The most likely explanation is earlier marriages and lengthier periods of child-bearing for wives, although this raises further questions of causation. At any rate, the pressure on the land grew both fast and steadily during the final third or so of the eighteenth century.

Food supplies were not at first a critical problem because of the spread of potato culture over almost the entire country; only in the north were cereals still an important part of the diet of the poorer peasants. The potato was remarkable for its ease of cultivation, return per acre and nutritional value if eaten in sufficient quantity. Nor was land-availability as yet an obstacle to earlier marriages and more families. It was in the landlords' interest to enlarge the volume of their rents. For most this was their primary, and for many their only, concern as proprietors, whether they let their land directly or through middlemen. Thus, so long as rents could be extracted from the cultivators at a higher rate, the land owners or managers generally encouraged the subdivision of holdings, and countenanced putting more and more marginal land into use. The increased demand for wheat, oats, barley and flax was a major activator of the process. Its prime beneficiaries were the aristocracy, gentry and middlemen. It was they who reaped most of the benefits of the increased national product. But, at least for the time being, the move to tillage (to crops) also helped to maintain the multiplying population, probably at a higher standard of living than that of the preceding generation. By 1791, moreover, war and with it soaring demand and prices for agricultural produce were already looming.

Concurrently, industry and trade, though very much smaller in scale, were generally expanding. Linen manufacture was particularly important both for its volume and because much of the spinning and weaving was done at home, supplementing farm income. Although by the last quarter of the eighteenth century north-east Ulster was the main centre of flax-growing and linen-making, these were also quite widespread in other regions. At this early stage in the Industrial Revolution, cotton, relying on water-powered spinning mills, was another Irish manufacture. Dublin, now a major European capital, was not only a flourishing commercial centre but had also developed skilled work forces, especially in the booming building industry and brewing and distilling. Cork too was advancing economically, as its international provisions and butter trades grew fast.

One must not paint too rosy a picture. The 'prosperity' of the 1780s and 1790s was strictly relative to what had gone before and what was to come. By no standard could it be regarded as absolute. The persistent agrarian disorders testified to the constant conflict brought about by rising rents, changes in land use and competition for holdings. Agricultural life for the mass of small tenants, cottiers and landless labourers was still nasty and brutish if not, by contemporary European standards, particularly short. A considerable proportion of the rural population—and at least 90 per cent of people dwelt outside the cities and large towns—lived in one-roomed cabins without chimneys or glazed windows, and often in the company of animals. Agricultural methods and implements were primitive. Iron (as against wooden) spades, forks and ploughshares, ploughing harness (as against attachment to horses' tails) and wheeled carts were still comparatively rare. Seed was usually poor, crop rotation ill-understood and ill-practised, and the dominant varieties of livestock were much inferior in size and return to their English counterparts. The modernised form of farming—the 'agricultural revolution'— making headway in the Scottish Lowlands and East Anglia particularly, in Ireland was confined to a few pockets of experimentation. Taking it all in all, however, the economic state of Ireland in 1791 compared favourably with that of most other years in the preceding century; and so it would have seemed to most contemporaries. They could not have been expected to discern the long-term weaknesses of the economy—the increasing rapidity of the population growth, the absence of significant coal and iron deposits that the next stage of industrialisation was to demand, and the reduction, and ultimately the abandonment, of agricultural protection in Great Britain on whose markets Irish exports were almost entirely dependent.

The social structure

Sea communications between Britain and Ireland were little better in 1800 than in 1700, but transport within Ireland improved remarkably, especially in the last quarter of the century. In the 1780s, coaches were introduced on the major routes, adding to and speeding up the network already provided by their stage counterparts. Travel time on these express services was sharply reduced. That for the Dublin–Belfast run, for instance, fell from two to three days at the beginning of the century to half a day by the end. Cheaper and slower public cars, some with fixed schedules, also began to ply over short distances, as between neighbouring towns. The prime reason for the improvement was the Irish Parliament's heavy expenditure on roads after 1750, in part to build up the economic infrastructure, in part to spend public revenue at home instead of remitting it to Britain, and in part to suit the interests and convenience of individual MPs. By 1791 Irish main roads, although much fewer in number, were probably superior in quality to English. They also gained from the comparative absence of heavy industrial and commercial traffic that quickly broke down the English surfaces. There was a correspondingly remarkable development of river navigation and canals in the late eighteenth century, particularly in the eastern part of the country, while work on clearing the Shannon, and linking it to Dublin was well under way.

These changes affected relatively few directly. Fares on all forms of public transport were extremely high, well over one penny per mile on even the longest runs. A labourer would have had to work for a week or more to earn enough to travel for fifty miles (80 km). At most, 20–30 000 persons per annum used the mail or stage coaches; fewer still could afford the very costly post-chaises or had private carriages or riding horses at their own command. Even a better-off farmer with a cart and workhorse of his own might take two or three days to travel to and from a market town twenty-five miles (40 kms) distant; it was not a journey he could undertake often. Thus, most Irish people rarely if ever moved beyond a radius of fifteen to twenty miles (15–32 km) from their homes; many lived within a still more circumscribed area. Correspondingly, marriages within the native locality were the norm.

Yet it must not be inferred that social life was thin and meagre or that the Irish countryside constituted so many square miles of introspective gloom. Even as early as 1791, on the eve of a further demographic explosion, the rural population was comparatively dense in most regions. In place of the isolated farmhouse and outbuildings now typical of the Irish landscape, cabins had tended to spring up in clusters, often with short distances between settlements. Commonly, people had many neighbours either directly at hand or within easy walking distance. There is abundant evidence that great poverty and starkness of life had not crushed their spirit, that gossip and storytelling, and dancing and singing, enlivened the evenings of even the lowest on the social ladder, those who lacked tenancies of any kind. Religious feasts, 'patterns' (the word derived from the festivities celebrating patron saints) and fairs were frequent, and with them games, athletic contests, drinking, hilarity and fighting. Even the innumerable beggars, the most inveterate foot-travellers of the day, were often described as good-humoured and witty as well as professionally eloquent.

Late eighteenth century Irish rural life was therefore crowded and vivacious rather than solitary and misanthropic as a rule. It was also marked by a high degree of mutuality. Most people were set in webs of inner and outer family kinship connections, and reciprocal help was often necessary and obedient to well-understood conventions in the poorer communities. Religion also provided important social as well as other sorts of bond, although, in the 1790s, the Catholic Church was only painfully and partially ridding itself of the penal shadows. Catholic recovery, in the full sense of regular mass-going, systematic devotions and a

20

fixed ecclesiastical structure, was as yet only beginning to emerge, even in sophisticated circles. In all but the most remote and least 'reformed' of regions, however, the priest's mission provided meeting-grounds for people and gradually reduced the pre-Christian elements in peasant culture.

There was some correlation between Catholic modernisation and the retreat of Gaelic as the spoken tongue. The Irish language had been in decline since, at latest, the mid-eighteenth century. By 1791, not much above half the population was monolingually Irish-speaking, although the number who spoke Irish as well as English was of course quite large. A century later less than 1 per cent was monolingually Irish-speaking, and even the proportion of bilingualists had fallen below 15 per cent. The fundamental reason for the decline in Gaelic, already well marked in the 1790s, was simply the desire to survive in the modern world, or better still to improve one's lot. English was virtually the sole language of administration, law, commerce and literacy; Gaelic was coming to be associated increasingly, in the popular mind, with poverty, struggle and distress. But though the primary cause of de-Gaelicisation was the desire to adapt to the modern world, the Church unconsciously facilitated the process by the use of English where practicable. It was not hostile to Irish as such; in fact, it supported in various ways the teaching of Irish to its priests. But its purpose was essentially utilitarian. Gaelic was a necessity where one's pastorate was still Irish-speaking. Otherwise English was used. Although things would be different a century later, most of the clergy in the 1790s probably shared the peasant attitude to the native language.

Education (mainly mathematical and classical in basis, where it extended beyond reading, writing and elementary arithmetic) was almost exclusively conducted in English. The regular schools were Anglican foundations for the most part, and the Presbyterians had their own well-developed system. Formal Catholic education as such scarcely existed as yet in Ireland; the few who could afford it sent their boys to be 'finished' in Continental seminaries. This did not mean that all Catholics (except for the Continental handful) were uneducated. Catholics formed the bulk of the pupils of the hedge schools (so called because they were often held in the open air in summer) and of the itinerant masters who made a circuit of the homes of substantial farmers. Such schools and teaching were not however denominational; boys of all religions in a neighbourhood might attend them. Their reputation—as it has descended to posterity at least—was extraordinarily high. There is much early nineteenth century testimony from former pupils who reached eminence of one sort or another as to the excellence of the grounding they received from hedge school or travelling masters. It is difficult to believe that the entire race of such instructors was gifted or could work effectively with few books and virtually no classroom comforts. But a high degree of individual teaching as well as instant and stern retribution for laziness were provided; and most students were (in modern jargon) 'highly motivated' in their eagerness to escape the meshes of ignorance and poverty.

This private 'system' seems to have been remarkably widespread. According to the census of 1841, nearly half the Irish males and nearly one-third of Irish females who had been of school age in the 1790s were literate. These figures probably give an inflated impression of the extent of primary education—particularly for the Catholic majority—in the late eighteenth century. But even with a considerable discount, they tell a story of fairly widespread elementary instruction among the less poverty-stricken farming classes, which in turn implies numerous hedge schools and travelling masters. Besides, literacy was not the only test of learning, or of mental or imaginative capacity. Ireland was famed for its oral tradition even then; and the Irish gift for language—especially dramatic, poetic and passionate language—owes much to the long-enforced reliance on the speaking tongue and verbal transmission of the native culture.

22

Gaelic literature was not yet quite dead. Even in the last third of the eighteenth century it yielded some remarkable poetry. But these were the final flickers of an exhausted fire. Anglo-Irish literature was about to kindle, at first chiefly in Maria Edgeworth's writings. It was she who delineated, in *Castle Rackrent,* what were—or were to become—stock Irish characters of peasantry and Ascendancy alike. Both stereotypes—the subtle, ironic, linguistically dextrous and prudently ambivalent peasant and the wild, brave, unfeeling, self-absorbed and overspending landlord—fit the framework of colonialism. Each was a caricature that would fit no single individual exactly. Yet it would be foolish to reject national characteristics as so much nonsense, particularly those that may plausibly be rooted in actual national situations. The Irish reaching Australia in 1791 and later years were different in certain measure from the other immigrants; and, from Irish governor down to illiterate transportee, part of this difference derived from the peculiarities of Ireland's political dependence and degradation.

2

Politics: 1791–1830

The impact of the French Revolution

Throughout the 1790s the French Revolution dominated the course of events in Ireland as well as elsewhere in Europe. It acted as a burning glass on all the hereditary antagonisms and anxieties, and speeded up new processes amazingly.

The inveterate problem of Protestant insecurity intensified as the Revolution became ever more radical and bloody. All too readily, the majority of the Anglo-Irish Ascendancy and their satellites saw themselves as cast in the same role as the French nobility and its support bodies. Increasingly, it seemed possible that a large-scale upheaval in Ireland would ultimately lead the governing class to the scaffold or guillotine, or at best to escape as desperate refugees stripped of possessions and prospects. Thus the advance towards the Terror in France was matched by the increase of anticipatory fears at home. These were exacerbated by the apparent undermining, at the insistence of the British government, of the Protestant Supremacy which had served so long—at least, in Protestant imaginations—as the planters' shield. In 1792 and again in 1793, Pitt and his Cabinet forced a reluctant Irish Parliament to pass further measures of Catholic relief. That of 1793 was especially alarming to Protestants for it both enfranchised Catholics, wherever they had the requisite parliamentary qualifications, and opened up to them hitherto exclusive professions and occupations.

It is true that even the 1793 Act was a highly qualified and, to Catholics, even an insulting concession. It created new animosities. For instance, Catholics were permitted to enter the junior but not the senior Irish Bar. They were allowed to vote in parliamentary elections but not for other Catholics: the prohibition against Catholics sitting in Parliament was maintained. Such compromises may have seemed politically necessary in order to leave the begrudging Ascendancy with the feeling that their inmost citadels remained intact; but they were politically disastrous in underlining yet again that Catholics were second-class citizens, and that their campaign for civic parity was still being baulked. In the short term at any rate, full and generous concession would have cost the Ascendancy little of their power or privilege; it would have been practically costless. Even if the government had wished it, no Catholic could have become a King's Counsel for many years to come for they had only just begun to practise at the Bar; and to throw Parliament open to all religions would have meant no more than a dozen or two Catholic peers or gentry MPs, probably more servile, if anything, than the rest. Such rational calculations, however, were very distant from people's minds in the midst of the growing turmoil.

During the following year, 1794, the antagonisms intensified. So too did the economic distress and dislocations flowing from wartime taxation and other exigencies. Internal order deteriorated as the country was denuded of troops for service overseas. This time they were replaced, not by 'citizen' Volunteers, but by an ill-disciplined militia which, despite many Catholics among the rank-and-file, was dominated by the right wing of the Ascendancy who were hell-bent on crushing 'subversion'. Meanwhile, one of the forms of agrarian conspiracy, Defenderism, was influenced by the new French Revolutionary ideas. The influence had oblique rather than direct effects. Defender radicalism

25

looked more to the triumph of the Catholic Church than to that of reason or fraternity, and more to some form of Stuart restoration than to any species of republic. None the less the objective had changed from the defence of threatened status or practices to the revolutionary overthrow of the existing order, and from primarily economic to primarily political ends.

This shift in emphasis began in the 'frontier' regions where Catholic and Protestant settlement overlapped, mainly along the Ulster border. It was also manifest in certain other areas such as north Wexford. Gradually it spread into Connacht and upper Leinster as well as into towns and even the capital itself. As usual, Catholic action bred Protestant reaction. The Oakboys and Peep-O'-Day Boys, the Protestant counterparts of the Defenders, were as committed to conspiratorial violence in support of their supremacy as were the Defenders to its destruction.

Repression also changed the character of the United Irishmen or at least accelerated their radicalisation. In May 1794 the Society was declared illegal. Already some of its members had begun to conspire for a French invasion. 'I was one of those', Tone later wrote, 'who, seeing all the danger and horror of a contest, still thought the independence of the country an object worth risking all to obtain.'[3] Through informers, the government was privy to the plot. In response it arrested a French agent (who committed suicide during his trial) and several leading members of the Society. Tone managed to strike an insincere bargain with Dublin Castle whereby he agreed to go into exile in the United States without revealing that he intended to return from America to France. The critical results of the suppression of the United Irishmen were to drive them underground as a secret, cellularly organised body; to forge links between them and the Defender groups; to redouble their intrigues with revolutionary France; and eventually, towards the end of 1796, to produce a French invasion through Tone's persistent advocacy of such a gamble from the moment that he set foot in Paris. Each step, made known to the Castle with some degree of accuracy (though also some inaccuracy) by its web of spies, steadily increased the fears and reactive brutality of the authorities.

Caught between rising potential violence on either side, the Irish moderates were a shrinking band, and fared ill. The 'reform' party in Parliament fell steadily in number from 1792 on. It was in a cleft stick. As Grattan afterwards summed it up,

> . . . we did not approve of the conduct of the United Men, and we could not approve of the conduct of the Government. We were afraid of encouraging the former by making speeches against the latter.[4]

Meanwhile, the cautious party among the Catholic leadership was both angry at its partial failure in 1793 and in danger of losing its influence over the Catholic masses. Suddenly, the whirligigs of British politics seemed to offer an escape route to both sets of moderates.

Late in 1794, Pitt was forced to enter a coalition with a section of the Whigs and, as part of the price of the alliance, to appoint the liberal Earl Fitzwilliam as Irish Lord-Lieutenant. On arrival, Fitzwilliam electrified Dublin by courting the support of Grattan and the other Irish 'reformers'. He went on to dismiss most of the senior officers of the Irish administration, and to cause bills providing for an almost complete Catholic Emancipation to be introduced in the Irish House of Commons. The subsequent furore, especially at the sweeping away of all the principal office holders in Dublin Castle, led Pitt to recall Fitzwilliam in disgrace within six weeks of his taking up his post. Historians usually stress the exorbitance of Fitzwilliam's behaviour. He certainly exceeded his implicit instructions and acted as if it were he, and not the government that appointed him, who was the determiner of policy. It is also true that he was anticipating by several decades what was ultimately bound to happen, and that the long postponement and increasing embitterment were to cost Britain very dearly.

The Fitzwilliam débâcle was the turning point of the 1790s in Ireland. From then on the Irish government committed itself completely to the course of repression while the various independent forces of violence (not least the newly founded Orange Order) hardened in their respective attitudes. Great bloodshed was now inevitable. It could well have come in 1796 had the French expeditionary force of December of that year succeeded in landing on the southwest coast. The expedition was well equipped, had 15 000 seasoned troops, enjoyed adequate naval support, was commanded by Bonaparte's brilliant young rival, Hoche, and was accompanied by Tone himself. Although Kenmare Bay, the place of disembarkation enforced by bad weather rather than chosen, was not in a strong Defender or United Irish region, Hoche's little army would probably have met no worthwhile resistance before reaching Cork, and perhaps not even before its north-eastern drive began to close on Dublin—having perhaps gathered considerable armed support on the way. Not altogether unreasonably, later commentators have had fantasies in which the expedition and its Irish allies overran the entire country and set up an Irish Republic à la other French satellite states. But the weather that drove the French fleet into Kenmare Bay also prevented it from landing any troops there. The venture failed totally without a shot being fired.

The narrowness of their escape aroused in the authorities a fresh frenzy of brutal counteraction. In the spring of 1797 petitioning and public meetings were prohibited and an offensive opened against the Belfast and other northern radicals. Over five hundred political arrests were made and thousands of farms and other buildings were searched, often with great savagery, for arms. Dublin Castle gave General Lake, the commander of the punitive army, *carte blanche* to stamp out sedition, and he responded by burning dwellings, and quartering troops wholesale on suspected households. These terrorising means substantially achieved their end. Although Ulster did produce United Irish outbreaks in 1798, they were on a much lesser scale than would have been thought likely two years before, and in the interval many of the potential rebels had changed their allegiance to Orangeism and support of the Crown against the Papists—for they now saw the primary Irish contest in these terms. By a similar process, the United Irish movement in the rest of Ireland was substantially Catholicised by the beginning of 1798. Even the oath to be administered became in places one requiring members 'to be true to the Catholic religion, and to assist the French should they land in this Kingdom'.

As Ulster was being disarmed, the government also arrested and interned most of the United Irish leaders outside the province, including the entire Leinster Directory of the Society. Thus, in certain senses, the Rising, when it came at last in May 1798, was not truly a United Irish rebellion, outside of Ulster. Although it is commonly so-called and in fact embraced many rank-and-file members of the Society, the surviving United Irish leadership in the south and west was too few in number and too poor in quality to initiate, harness or give direction to the popular outbreak in Wexford. The major Wexford uprising of 1798 had some nationalistic and libertarian objectives of a general kind; but it was mainly a protective movement sparked off by military oppression of the type to which Ulster had already been subjected, and by the panic actions of local Orangemen and proprietors. After its initial success, the revolt spread to the adjoining counties, especially Carlow and Wicklow; so too did the dreadful atrocities committed by both sides. The sectarian element also was increasingly evident. Despite some able leadership, the rebels, without French support or modern armament, could not possibly hold out for long, and on 21 May 1798 were routed in their last stand on Vinegar Hill, close to the places in Wexford where it had all begun. New South Wales was to have its own Vinegar Hill, with a similar result, a few years later.

The uprising was probably the most sanguinary episode in all Irish history. The total mortality may have been as high as 30 000—to say nothing of all other sufferings and destruction. It immediately entered the historical consciousness and mythology on each side of the great Irish divide. The Protestant origins of and participation in the insurrection were immediately slurred over and, as far as possible, obliterated from the memory of their side. Instead, 1798 became a symbol (to take its place with the 'massacre' of new Protestant settlers in Ulster in 1641) of the Papists' ineradicable savagery and treachery, and a further argument for 'No Surrender' on Protestant supremacy. Its place in the Catholic mind was more complex. Here, 1798 both identified Catholicism with separatism *and* stressed the Protestant element in the uprising as proof that the Irish nation consisted, in Tone's phrase, of 'Protestant, Catholic and Dissenter' bound together by a common birthplace and a common necessity 'to break the connection with England, the never-failing source of all our political evils'. If there were contradictions between these standpoints, they were disregarded.

Similarly ambivalent was the legacy of the bloodshed. On the one hand, it created or confirmed in that great Catholic champion of 1805–47, Daniel O'Connell, a deep abhorrence of the use of physical force which he impressed on Irish nationalism for almost half a century. In reaction to the violence of the Wexford rising, O'Connell inaugurated a constitutional and peaceful tradition in Irish politics that was quite as powerful in its effects as that of the resort to arms. On the other hand, 1798 became a model for Irish republicans, as well as a golden link in the heroic chain of armed resistance to oppression that was to stretch to 1916 and, in some eyes, down to the present day. Moreover, O'Connell's 'peaceful' agitations of the 1820s and 1830s were to be stiffened by former United Irishmen and rebels, in much the same way as Parnell's agitations of the 1880s were to gain from the work of ex-Fenians and other one-time revolutionaries. Finally, the 1798 rising made several contributions to the infant colony of New South Wales. It landed some 700 convicts, supposed to have participated in the rising, on its shores, and began or crystallised two major opposing traditions in the colonial ideology. One was the anti-authoritarian and anti-British strain; the other, a profound fear and distrust of the Irish and their supposed conspiratorial practices.

Union!

The natural response to the rebellion, and the scenes of horror that accompanied and succeeded it, was—according to English orthodoxy—a union between the two kingdoms. Incorporation should help to secure Ireland militarily, and the Irish sectarian problem should be much reduced, if not altogether resolved, by being placed in a much larger and more 'civilized' social and religious context. However, the uprising was more the occasion than the cause of the British government's decision in late 1798 to press ahead with constitutional amalgamation. Six years earlier Pitt had confided to the Irish Lord-Lieutenant, 'a union with this country has long been in my mind'. It was the intractable difficulty of trying to govern Ireland with a quasi-independent and often fractious Irish Parliament that had driven Pitt to this conclusion. After 1793 he was confirmed in his opinion by the patent danger of being linked to a country perpetually on the verge of civil war while he conducted a life-and-death struggle with revolution on the Continent.

There was no significant British opposition to the proposed union. The equivalent union between England and Scotland in 1707 was generally deemed successful and a hopeful precedent; and direct rule appealed to busy statesmen and administrators who assumed that the judicious exercise of untrammelled power would soon reduce Ireland

31

to order and rationality. Moreover, the exigencies of war seemed to demand bold, simple measures. The only certain way to prevent Ireland being used as the backdoor for an invasion of Britain was to become doorkeeper oneself, instead of sharing the duty with a jittery and minor partner. There was remarkably little—perhaps even no—serious consideration at either Westminster or Whitehall of how the political junction was to work in practice. Detail was simply disregarded. In the crisis of European war, British politicians plunged for what looked like a once-for-all and immediate solution to a most pressing problem. The future could take care of itself.

A considerable part, perhaps even the majority, of the Irish Ascendancy took a different view. A few, like John Fitzgibbon (now Lord Clare), had believed for some time that their only long-term security lay in a fusion with Great Britain, and the traumas of 1795–98 had driven many others into the same camp. Even so, Irish Protestant anti-unionists still abounded in 1799. They were by no means all liberals or radicals but included some of the wealthiest and most conservative noblemen, landlords and officials. For the union seemed to threaten important established interests. It would obliterate two-thirds of the seats in the Irish House of Commons, most of them boroughs wholly or partly 'owned' by the great proprietors. It might also strike at various forms of Irish commerce, crafts and manufacture, and would undoubtedly reduce Dublin's social and economic significance. And the Irish Bar faced a decline in its most lucrative business. More generally, the Parliament at College Green was seen as the strongest bulwark against Catholic pretensions, while Westminster was suspected of being all too ready to sell out on this issue if subjected to heavy pressure. This feeling was particularly strong in the Orange Order, whose loyalty to Britain had been, from the start, conditional. The Orange Oath promised only to 'defend the king and his heirs *as long as* [my italics] he or they support the protestant ascendancy'.

32

Conversely, the Irish Catholic Church was seduced by the tacit promise of complete emancipation. When this prospect was dangled before them, the great majority of educated Irish Catholics and their organisations, and almost the entire Irish Catholic episcopate, became strong supporters of the projected union. They felt no loyalty whatever to an Irish Parliament traditionally hostile to their advance. As ever, they saw the British government as offering their best hope of relief. The future Catholic champion, O'Connell, then a recently called barrister of 24, pressed the opposite policy. Publicly he proclaimed distrust of Britain, resistance to the union, and reliance on his Protestant fellow-Irishmen for justice—ultimately. His was almost a solitary voice in 1800. He was one of only a handful of Catholics to call for the continuance of Ireland's independent legislature; even his own uncles and brothers were vehement pro-unionists.

Although Catholic support was very valuable to Pitt, it was Irish parliamentary support that was indispensable, for the union Bill had been defeated when first introduced in the Irish House of Commons in 1799. Dublin Castle set about reversing this vote by the usual Castle means. Votes were purchased by the grant of pensions, peerages, places and even, in a handful of cases, plain money. Such an intervention was not particularly shocking to contemporaries. Politics were commonly 'managed' in such a way and parliamentary seats regarded as the saleable property of those who controlled them. The scale of the government's expenditure, and the profusion of its distribution of honours and favours, were, however, unprecedented. They were also ample for their purpose. A modified union Bill passed the Irish House of Commons with comparative ease (158 votes to 115) in the following year. In the Irish House of Lords the margin was over two to one.

O'Connell wrote later of his anguish and despair when on 1 January 1801 he heard the bells of Dublin ringing in the welcome to the new United Kingdom. To him, it was the celebration of a national humiliation. His condemnation proved justified—at least insofar as the British government failed to couple the union with emancipation. The influence of Dublin Castle, combined with the anti-Catholic forces in high politics in London, English opinion at large and, in particular, George III's refusal to countenance the overthrow (as he saw it) of the Protestant supremacy that he had sworn to uphold, were too powerful for Pitt to carry the expected measure of Catholic relief. He resigned as Prime Minister but this merely confirmed the Catholic defeat. Conversely, the same defeat transformed the great majority of Irish Protestants into supporters of the union. The *fait accompli* switched their point of view. Quite suddenly, their only real safety seemed to lie in absorption into a greater British state.

A descent into provincialism was one price they had to pay, almost immediately. Dublin rapidly lost its standing as a genuine European capital. It was soon largely deserted by the aristocracy and the landed rich, with social leadership falling more and more into the hands of resident merchant princes, barristers and physicians. The 'season' dwindled to a few weeks centred on the vice-regal 'court' between January and March. The general population of the capital ceased to grow significantly and the formerly flourishing building and decorative trades had to find new customers, largely in the churches. Now and then, in special crises, even as late as the 1830s, unemployment and diminished status led disgruntled Dublin Protestants to grumble against the union. But they always fled back to its supposed protection once the opposite and apparently much greater evil of a Catholic-dominated Ireland rose again before their eyes.

For the Irish upper classes the centre of gravity shifted increasingly to Great Britain. Many of the wealthiest lived there, at least for a considerable period of the year, and sent their sons to English schools and universities. Even the less affluent resident Irish landowners were generally affected by the higher living standards that British models tempted them to imitate, often with disastrous consequences for their fortunes. By a double retrogressive process, the post-union Ascendancy tended to become once more alienated from their country of residence and to redefine themselves as a sort of imperial garrison.

Thus the union led quite rapidly to a fresh alignment of Irish allegiances. The great majority of Catholics were transformed into nationalists and anti-unionists of varying degrees of intensity and extremity. Even the Catholic gentry and well-to-do middle classes sufficiently resented the multiple forms of inferiority still imposed on them to share in these feelings to some degree. Correspondingly, Irish Protestants drew together. Some continued and sometimes sharp conflict between the established and nonconforming churches was inevitable, given the increasingly hot religious fervour of the day. But when political danger—which can be taken to mean, in Irish circumstances, the prospect of Catholic domination—appeared on the horizon, Protestants generally made common cause.

There would always be some Protestant anti-unionists. In fact, at least half of the front rank of the nationalist leadership in the nineteenth century was Protestant in faith. Equally there would always be, even in the years before emancipation, some 'Castle Catholics', pro-unionists from conviction or innate conservatism, or drawn in that direction by social aspiration or the hope of gain. Nevertheless, the Act of Union had redrawn the Irish lines of battle in an essentially sectarian way. Henceforth, political leaning ordinarily depended on religion. In nineteen cases out of twenty (or often even more) one's attitude to the constitutional union with Great Britain depended on whether, as a Catholic, one saw it as a barrier to advancement and a distortion of identity or, as a Protestant, one saw it as the ultimate security of position, possessions and self-esteem.

The economic effects of the union were less clear-cut. It was to become a catchword among later nationalists that the union was responsible for Ireland's impoverishment and helplessness in the nineteenth century. Certain trends were, however, more an implication of the relative physical situation of the two islands than the result of any political settlement. For example, long before the Act of Union, Britain had begun to predominate in Irish trade. By 1800 over 85 per cent of Irish exports were to Britain, and nearly 80 per cent of Irish imports were of British origin. One country was industrialising fast and possessed great quantities of the two essential natural resources for the next stage of the Industrial Revolution—coal and iron. The other could not compete in most modern manufactures and was practically devoid of the necessary minerals. One led the world in per capita investment capital. The other was low even on the European scale. It was, if not inevitable, at least highly likely that, whatever the political arrangements, Ireland's economy would be subordinated to Britain's needs for markets for its manufactured goods and agricultural produce to feed its rapidly growing urban population.

On the other hand, the Irish economy suffered directly from the union in at least two significant respects. First, after 1800 Ireland was liable for a fixed proportion of the joint national debt, and this soared to undreamt-of heights during the war years, 1801–15. Second, Ireland's economic plight, in so far as it was considered seriously in the first quarter of the nineteenth century, was considered in a Parliament and by a Cabinet dominated by British viewpoints and interests; the old Irish Parliament which had been abolished in 1801 at least knew of its own country's conditions at first hand, and had a certain stake in their amelioration. Later on, the economic consequences of British domination were more mixed. But the first stage of the union was marked by crude and often disastrous attempts to force British norms of propertied and commercial relations upon a structure to which they were largely foreign.

Yet the potentiality to force Britain to listen to Irish complaint, and attend sooner or later to Irish need, was also implicit in the union. Irish disorder was now a direct British responsibility. The revolutionary movement, which reached its highest point in the United Irishmen, was not a grave immediate problem after 1800. Although the young Robert Emmet and his followers did attempt another rising in Dublin in 1803, it was an unlucky and bungled affair of minute proportions, however much it added to later nationalist rhetoric and legend. Nor was agrarian unrest really threatening to the social order between the passage of the Act of Union and the conclusion of the Napoleonic War. After 1815, however, with the collapse of agricultural prices when peace arrived, rural intimidation and conspiracy returned in force, particularly to Munster. The specifically political element was, once again, comparatively insignificant in the labourers' and small farmers' movements; their prime concern was to turn back the economic clock or at least hold still its hands. By the early 1820s many thousands were involved in or subject to the dictates of the secret societies; violence was becoming endemic once again in the 'disturbed' counties. For good or ill, British legislators and administrators could not long escape the conclusion that Ireland demanded special measures—even beyond the degree to which it was already a special case.

Although the 100 Irish members in the House of Commons at Westminster were outnumbered by more than five to one, they were at least now situated at the real centre of political power. Initially, they constituted little more than a handful of new recruits for the established British political groupings. In the general election of 1818, however, signs began to appear that Irish county electorates could be influenced by forces other than government, bribery or landlords. In particular, it was shown that candidates, in a number of the comparatively large constituencies, could be forced to declare themselves on the issue of emancipation, and risk rejection if they failed to satisfy Catholic electors. There was even some evidence of organised Catholic pressure and, here and there, of priests helping to mobilise the

Catholic tenant vote. From these very small beginnings, an independent Irish membership in the House of Commons was to develop with surprising speed. Within fifteen years, this membership was sufficient to form a considerable party, quite disciplined by contemporary standards. It was to prove capable of opposing, fairly systematically, any government whose official policy on an Irish issue was abhorrent. This unlooked for consequence of a united parliament produced a new and most unwelcome factor in the trafficking of the House of Commons and eventually provided a certain measure of Irish leverage over British Cabinets.

The Catholic question

In the long run, it was the Catholic issue that was critical in bringing about the new sort of United Kingdom politics. Although Ireland was the natural arena for the fight for emancipation, it was several years after the Act of Union before a really effective offensive was mounted there. The most basic problem for its Catholic proponents was, as usual, a division in both leadership and strategy. For long, one party advocated the acceptance of the 'securities' proposed by British sympathisers—state payment of the Catholic clergy and state control over at least the highest Catholic ecclesiastical appointments—in order to ease the passage of emancipation through the imperial parliament and past the conscientious scruples of George III. The other, more numerous, popular and vociferous party, dominated by Daniel O'Connell and supported by a number of other Catholic barristers, demanded the immediate and unconditional grant of emancipation. At first, the Irish bishops, still in the grip of the old servility, backed the conservative Catholic lobby. But from 1808 on O'Connell harried them ceaselessly in public; and by 1815, through a mixture of forthrightness, flattery and intimidation (and chiefly the last) he had swung them almost *en bloc* to his side. In that year Catholic hopes were dimmed by Bonaparte's final defeat at

Waterloo. As O'Connell clearly recognised, the British Cabinet's incentive to mollify discontented Irish Catholics and appease Continental Catholic interests disappeared when the French no longer threatened international order.

From 1808 on, O'Connell had been the heart and soul of the Irish Catholic movement; but after 1815 he had to maintain the campaign almost single-handed, amid the utmost apathy. While he himself never faltered, as late as 1822 it still seemed near-hopeless. Another persistent weakness in the Catholic movement was its relative failure to harness its main force—the sheer weight of Catholic numbers and the scale of their majority in Ireland—to the cause. O'Connell had made considerable progress in political organisation in Dublin, Cork, Limerick and the larger towns in Leinster and Munster, especially those that he and fellow Catholic barristers regularly visited on their twice-yearly circuits. He had also fought major political cases in the courts, which had won his cause much publicity and many partisans; and he worked tirelessly at propaganda. Nevertheless, he had produced no more than an intermittently threatening pressure group which, by the early 1820s, seemed to have exhausted itself in a succession of fruitless agitations.

The Catholic Association instituted in 1823 by O'Connell and another brilliant Catholic advocate, R. L. Sheil, eventually transformed this situation. In former years, Sheil had been a leading light of the more conservative Catholic party, and his conjunction with O'Connell signalled the beginning of the end of the old division. Gradually, O'Connell introduced the three novel elements that were to make the new agitation truly formidable. First, he extended the range of the Association's business to include discrimination of almost every kind against Catholics, and opposed the inequities in the press and courts alike: this greatly widened the movement's appeal. Next, by converting the powerful and eloquent Bishop James Doyle of Kildare and Leighlin to his cause, he managed to enlist, by the end of 1824, the support of the great majority of the Irish Catholic prelates, parish priests and other clergy: the Church provided an unrivalled organisational network over most of the country as well as an invaluable moral sanction and sense of righteous crusade for what was essentially a sectional undertaking. Last but by no means least, he opened the Association to the rural masses by reducing their subscription, popularly called a 'rent', to one farthing a week. This meant that, where the Association caught on, vast numbers felt themselves to have a vital interest in its operation, with correspondingly high expectations and campaigning fervour.

A further ingredient of success was added by another young member of the Association, Thomas Wyse, who was the first to grasp the full possibilities of using the Catholic tenant vote to increase the pressure for emancipation. The organisational work that he inspired in Co. Waterford before the general election of 1826 was imitated in five other county constituencies—to such effect that half-a-dozen MPs, committed to full emancipation, were then returned against the wishes of the respective landlord interests. These victories made a deep impression on major British politicians, especially the two tory leaders, Sir Robert Peel and the Duke of Wellington. The hold of proprietors on their tenants' votes was one of the staple elements of the entire governmental system, and the 1826 election had shown that it could be broken by the conjoined influence of the 'demagogues' and Romish clergy, an Irish combination to be dreaded. O'Connell himself delivered the *coup de grace* when in 1828 he stood for a by-election in Co. Clare and, with the fervent support of the priests and the entire Catholic movement, including even its small aristocratic wing, trounced his landlord-supported opponent by a majority of more than three to one.

The British government was trapped. As a Catholic, O'Connell was prohibited from entering Parliament. Yet it was now clear that the majority of Irish county constituencies both could and would place Catholic candidates at the top of the poll in by-elections and general elections. More-over, Catholic Ireland was now in a high state of excitement, and civil war seemed a distinct possibility as armed Prot-estant counterforces were established and the Association found it more and more difficult to restrain menacing demonstrations by its own mass following. Early in 1829 Wellington and Peel cut the Gordian knot by concluding that full emancipation must be granted—the use of the army to repress the Irish Catholics by force presented too many dangers and uncertainties. By threats of resignation, they then compelled their colleagues and ultimately the King himself to bow to the inevitable. The *Roman Catholic Relief Act* of 1829 disenfranchised the main body of the Catholic electors, the small tenant farmers holding 40s. freeholds, and contained several other clauses designed to abase Catholics in minor, generally symbolic, matters. But this was regarded as a trivial price to pay—in fact, in the case of the disenfranchisement a price welcomed by some of the Catholic leaders—for a great triumph of popular organisa-tion over official power.

The struggle for and attainment of Catholic emancipation was of critical importance in Irish history—and, by exten-sion, of considerable importance to Australia, too. The campaign had provided a long and difficult but ultimately profitable lesson in how to promote and manage agitation. The *Relief Act* itself directly benefited only a minute pro-portion of the Irish Catholics, chief among them professional men like O'Connell himself; and even in the case of this class, there were still many hurdles to be cleared before formal parity could be translated into actual equality of opportunity. Even for the still-downtrodden mass of Catho-lics, the Act had a profound symbolic significance. It was long since Irish Catholics had been able to claim any triumph or feel any sense of their own power or worth. Above all, it was a victory won by their own exertion.

More concretely, the education of the Irish masses in constitutional and parliamentary politics had begun.

O'Connell was easily the most important in inculcating political values into, and organising the political participation of, the people at large; and this had been deliberately, if gradually, designed. Initially, during 1808–20, his use and deployment of the 'crowd' as a political force had been practically confined to Dublin and the larger urban centres of the south. It would have been difficult to muster quickly great numbers of rural dwellers for immediate action, as one crisis followed hard upon another. It might well have been impossible, as the priests, who were vital to rural organisation, were still largely neutral at this stage. But the Catholic Association of 1823 was to rest primarily on the peasantry and in particular on the 'Catholic rent' of one penny a month as the engine of their involvement.

Formal membership in the Association, sealed by the payment of the 'rent', engendered a commitment to the movement, as well as a sense of political manhood and self-respect. Wyse, the most profound and perceptive analyst of the Association, commented thus upon the weekly farthing subscription:

> The contribution was for *palpable* and *direct* purposes, purposes intelligible to and felt by the entire people: the connexion between the *tax* and the *benefit* was understood; it was not levied, but offered; it was voluntary, and not forced. It increased singularly the momentum of that impetus which the Association had now communicated to the entire body . . . Every farthing paid added a link to the chain; the contributors were the creditors, and the creditors were necessarily the partisans of the Association.[5]

Mass participation had much more than psychological and emblematic value. Just as the Whiteboys had tried to do in a different context and for different purposes, O'Connell used the force of numbers and communal solidarity for his particular ends. He was seeking, in general terms, to intimidate the British government by the spectacle of hundreds of thousands of poor and desperate men, barely held in leash by a moderate leadership. Again in general terms, the surrender of Peel and Wellington in 1828–29 marked the success of his strategy, for it was the fear of mass disorder and civil war that moved the ministers and their government to yield. Meanwhile, through enrolments for meetings, demonstrations and parliamentary petitions and as a support army for the electors, O'Connell went on mobilising more and more of the rural masses of Munster and Leinster politically.

Perhaps the most remarkable feature of all was the speed and ease with which the local priests could construct and manage large and complex county political machines. Part of the explanation is that they were dealing with voters habituated to acting under another sort of direction, that of landlords. Part lay in the fact that the structure of parish organisation and the weekly mass could be used, immediately and unchanged, for the formation of the political branches, the raising of revenue, and the promotion of public meetings and demonstrations of numerical strength. The entry of the priests into campaigning brought with it a new degree of sectarian bitterness, as well the preaching of a species of *jihad* which successfully fused the racial, tribal and religious appeals.

> You have heard the tones of the tempter and the charmer, (Father Tom Maguire roared to the tenants of Vesey Fitzgerald, O'Connell's opponent, at the polling booth in Ennis, Co. Clare, in 1828), whose confederates have through all ages joined the descendants of the Dane, the Norman, and the Saxon, in burning your churches, in levelling your altars, in slaughtering your clergy, in stamping out your religion. Let every renegade to God and his country follow Vesey Fitzgerald, and every true Catholic Irishman follow me.[6]

Thus the deliberate cultivation of Catholic grievances by O'Connell's Association and the intensity of the final struggle for emancipation deepened the denominational divide. Although O'Connell and most of his lieutenants intended no such outcome, it was implicit in their ceaseless efforts at 'consciousness-raising' among their co-religionists. Nothing touched Protestant fears more deeply than the prospect of 'the priest-in-politics'. It is true that in 1830 the Irish episcopate formally eschewed any further political participation and enjoined all priests to confine themselves strictly to their priestly functions. But it was now too late to turn back the clock. The Church had been integrated into the very structure of Irish agitation. To a very considerable extent, political division in the future was also to be religious division.

Meanwhile, two other developments in the years 1800–30 had already exacerbated religious antagonism in Ireland. One was a wave of Protestant missionary endeavour. This had most success initially in the remote Irish-speaking regions of the south-west. The other was the modernisation of the Catholic Church, with its accompaniment of church building, clerical discipline and order, regular Sunday mass-going, devotions and confraternities. This had most success initially in urban areas and their vicinities, and the less poverty-stricken and more English speaking parts of Leinster and Munster. In the end, Protestant evangelisation had limited effect whereas by the 1860s Catholic modernisation covered almost all the country. In the interval, however, bitter passions were aroused and Irish Protestantism, of all kinds, turned in an evangelical, and markedly biblical direction while Irish Catholicism became more triumphalist and Romanised, decade by decade.

One must not paint an altogether black picture of denominational distrust and hatred. After all, for most of the time most people over most of Ireland managed to live in tolerable harmony, if not positive amity, with members of other religions. In the early nineteenth century, banks, to take one example, were staffed almost exclusively by members of the Church of Ireland, yet the bulk of their small customers, outside the north-east, were Catholics. Similarly, Guinness was a 'Protestant' firm yet the great majority of the publicans who sold their product (to say nothing of the consumers) were Catholics. It is true that even in these cases, there were attempts to set up Catholic counter-institutions and counter-products in the strife-ridden 1820s and 1830s. But on the whole business relationships and the ordinary courtesies and accommodations of commercial life continued to override confessional differences. Again, sport, especially that centred on horses, could straddle the religious chasm on occasions. As the ballad *Galway Races* concluded with warm-hearted exaggeration:

> There was half a million people there of all denominations.
> The Catholic, the Protestant, the Jew and Presbetarian.
> There was yet no animosity, no matter what persuasion.
> But *failte* and hospitality, inducing fresh acquaintance.

Still, it is undeniable that Irish society became increasingly intolerant in the years immediately following the union, and that even in the quietest times there was deep latent hostility, requiring only some sparks of fear to be set aflame.

How the union turned out

Thus in many ways the union turned out very differently from the intended purposes of its authors. It was meant to reconcile the political and governmental systems of the two islands. Instead, there developed an irreconcilable opposition to British domination of Ireland, and this was soon to find a place at the very heart of the British system, the House of Commons. Moreover, Irish government, centred in and popularly known as Dublin Castle, was now more isolated and alien than ever. Again, the union was meant to produce a common national allegiance in which Irishness would be no more than a regional variation of the essentially British identification of all the inhabitants of the conjoined kingdoms. The fate of Welshness and Scottishness was the hopeful model for the union's visionaries. But it turned out otherwise in Ireland. Even those Irish people whose British identification intensified after the union (almost all of whom were Protestants) tended towards a conditional rather than an absolute loyalty. Britain was now their bulwark; if this weakened so would their degree of commitment to the United Kingdom. Yet again, the economic fusion that the union implied meant in practice a still greater subordination of Ireland to British interests, in the first half of the nineteenth century, at least. Finally, and most important of all in terms of the immediate reasons for the passage of the Act of Union, the aim of defusing the Irish Catholic issue by rendering Irish Catholics a harmless and safely indulged minority within a much greater polity failed altogether. Not only did the union disappoint Catholic expectations but also, over nearly thirty years, this disappointment increasingly embittered the relations between the sects and turned them into deeply inimical and effectively organised political camps.

3

Economy and society in the early nineteenth century

The economy in crisis

Possibly the religio-political conflict in Ireland would have been more muted and of much smaller dimensions had not the Irish economy fallen into ever greater difficulties once the Napoleonic Wars had ended. As things were, however, employment, incomes and, for the most destitute fifth of the population, even the chances of physical survival declined sharply after 1815. In the subsequent struggle to maintain a social footing, privileged positions were fiercely clung to, or fiercely resented, depending on which party occupied them. Agriculture was, of course, the principal resource, and the immediately pre-famine years were the critical period of the most extraordinary epoch in Irish farming. Both before and after this phase (1780–1850), the Irish agrarian economy was dominated by the raising of animals and the production and processing of animal products. But in the intervening seventy years the emphasis was increasingly on tillage and labor-intensive forms of cultivation. The high corn prices of wartime quickened this trend and by 1815 it was self-perpetuating. The initial rapid growth in population itself ensured, under existing conditions, a further and faster enlargement, the dangerous implications of which were fully apparent by 1830. By then,

Irish farm holdings amounted to some 700 000, almost three times as many as today. Fully three-quarters of the holdings, at less than twenty acres (8 ha), were not viable in any modern sense except that their wretched occupiers continued somehow or other to survive. Over half the holdings were in fact 4 hectares or less.

The pressure of population on resources after 1815 also led to a great and rapid expansion of the cottier class. Cottiers were a species of penniless entrepreneurs, who in effect rented the means of subsistence, the cabin and the potato patch, a cow or cows or pasture, from the farmers, and paid for them principally by labour. The element of speculation in the cottier's situation was his gamble that the yield from what he rented would provide his family with the means of life for twelve months. In these desperate gambles the odds against the cottier were already long in 1830, partly because the terms on which he took his patch were worsening with the rising competition of his fellows, and partly because the quality of his mainstay, the potato, was declining while reliance upon it for survival gradually increased. Still more miserable than the cottier's condition was that of the casual or unbound labourer, whether he took conacre (i.e. seasonal letting of a plot already prepared for cultivation), or attempted to live by his earnings, or intermingled both expedients. This class also grew fast in the postwar years. Worse still, the decline of weaving and of local small-scale handicrafts and manufacture from the late 1820s onwards threw large numbers of new landless labourers on the market.

As one form of economy hastened to its doom, the faint outlines of its eventual successor became discernible. But the effects of the political and economic mastery of Ireland by an industrialising Britain had not yet gone far enough to revolutionise Irish agriculture. For if the ultimate implication for Irish agriculture of the political union with Great Britain was to gear it to the British market and to increase the attractions of capitalistic forms of farming, it was very difficult, initially, to act upon this implication. Most Irish landlords lacked the money, knowledge and liberty of action to pursue such a course. Much of their land was in the hands of middlemen, who had been granted either ninety-nine year leases or leases for three lives in the late eighteenth century, and middlemen bled their temporary possessions white and invested nothing in the land. On the contrary, for short-term monetary gain, they often subdivided holdings freely, and for the sake of peace accepted widespread squatting. Even where the landowner still retained direct control, he had to move towards clearance or consolidation slowly and stealthily if he wished to avoid peasant counteraction. For that matter, he rarely possessed the ready capital to invest significantly in permanent improvement, for by the 1830s much of the Irish landed class was, at its own level, scarcely less beggared and debt-encumbered than the cottiers.

Paradoxically, the area of land cultivated, the amount of cereals grown, the number of animals raised and the quantity of animal products processed were all apparently on the increase from 1800 on. To some extent, these increases signified the coming of capitalistic and export-directed farming. But much more were they the signs of a final effort of the old agrarian economy to keep resources abreast of population by more tillage and labor-intensive activity. As population pressed more heavily upon resources, more and more wasteland was drawn into production. When prices fell or rents rose or both happened simultaneously, it was necessary to produce, by all possible means, more marketable goods to meet inescapable cash needs. Initially, the gap might be covered by a reduction in the standard of living, but there was a final limit (very close in hundreds of thousands of cases by 1830) to the degree to which reduced standards of life could meet the shortfall. As large numbers of people, or their children, were pressed down to lower and lower levels on the social scale, it was only to be expected that more potatoes should be grown, that marginal bog or mountain land should come under the spade, and that pig-raising (pigs were the main 'cash' crop of the poor) should become more intensive and the volume of bacon and pork products greater.

As has been said, the agricultural revolution of the early nineteenth century was having some effect even in pre-famine Ireland. By the 1820s and 1830s the iron plough was beginning to replace the wooden in most places, and the scythe the sickle. Green crops and modern crop rotation and diversification were becoming more common. Strains were gradually improved in all livestock—mainly by a dramatic shortening of the period of maturation. The new farming practices did not generally involve the numerous lower agrarian classes, except perhaps, over time, in live-stock strains. They touched only a minority of even the gentry and substantial farmers, and were much less developed and systematic than their British equivalents. In 1830—indeed as late as 1845—they were important more as the portents of a future order than as a major factor in current production. It was the doom implicit in the old order rather than the early intimations of what lay ahead that contemporaries rightly emphasised, although they might also have noted the desperate ingenuity with which Irish society reorganised itself to stave off mass starvation for as long as possible. Meanwhile, ominously, the part-failure of the potato crop in 1822, and increasingly in later seasons, was generally accompanied by partial famine. These were pre-monitory indications of the ultimate disaster.

The potato was the key indicator of Irish economic health, and the increase in its production after 1815 sig-nalled not prosperity but distress. It represented at once the facilitator and the consequence of a rising population. By 1830 the proportion of cottiers' and labourers' income that had to be devoted to renting potato land already exceeded 50 per cent; potato quality was steadily declining; and the summer hunger gap was becoming longer. The social weight hanging from a single root crop was growing heavier year by year. For the bulk of the rural population it was practically impossible to make further savings from reductions in their standard of living. Over 40 per cent lived in single-room mud cabins, and over 35 per cent more almost as miserably, except for a second or third room. Clothes, particularly for children, were often mere rags, and furnishings and utensils few and makeshift, with some households quite bereft. Any savings to be made in diet had perforce been made much earlier. The upper one-fifth, farmers with holdings of 15 acres (6 ha) and upwards, were more secure in every mode of life, but even their lot was increasingly precarious as labour-intensive cultivation was being pressed out in favour of land-intensive stock-raising, and the competition for tenancies grew ever sharper.

Pre-famine society

One consequence of the mounting pressure on resources was an Irish countryside very different from that of today. With about five times as great a density of rural population, and much bogland and mountainside brought under meagre cultivation, it must have borne more resemblance to an equatorial delta settlement than to any modern European agricultural community. Decade by decade, the packed cabins and crazy collections of roofs, huddled together to form the innumerable centreless hamlets, induced still greater gregariousness and more intense familial and local loyalties. These were manifested *inter alia* by frequent holidays, fairdays and other communal celebrations and gatherings, and also, conversely, by faction fights with fists, sticks and stones. Even licit whisky was very cheap, and this great alleviator of misery was consumed in great quantities by all except the poorest classes.

The early nineteenth century censuses classified some 20 per cent of the Irish population as urban dwellers. In many ways this was misleading for all settlements of twenty houses or more were placed in the 'urban' category. Thus, over 700 of the so-called 'urban districts' enumerated were populated by less than 500 people, and only eighteen Irish towns had populations in excess of 10 000. No place other than Dublin was as yet even close to 100 000, and Dublin itself still held well below one quarter of a million inhabitants. All the cities and towns, with the exception of Belfast and a handful of new junctions or termini of the road and canal systems, were growing much more slowly than the rural hinterland. Even Dublin grew by less than 15 per cent in the first forty years after the Act of Union.

Thus down to the Great Famine of 1845–52 more than nine out of ten Irish persons lived either in the crowded countryside or very small settlements or villages, and Irish emigration was correspondingly dominated by rural or near-rural dwellers. This form of rural living did not mean rural isolation. There cannot have been many country dwellers whose nearest neighbours were more than a few hundred metres away. It was the furthest possible cry from a scattered frontier type of existence. It mattered greatly, however, which particular parts of Ireland people lived in. Broadly speaking, the eastern half of the country (drawing the line, say, between the cities of Derry and Cork) was the more 'modernised'. One index of this was the continued rapid advance of English as the language in common use. By the mid-nineteenth century, Gaelic—and even the capacity to speak Gaelic—had disappeared from most of Leinster, most of Ulster and the northern and eastern areas of Munster, except for the westward side of Clare. In the main, the more English-speaking the region, the less impoverished it was. Very small holdings, very oppressive terms of tenure, and primitive methods of cultivation were most evident in Connacht and along the rest of the western and south-western seaboard. There the land was usually the poorest, boggiest and most mountainous; there the rainfall was usually the heaviest, want most acute and the threat of hunger sharpest. All this reinforced the existing popular, and indeed general, association of poverty with the Irish language, and the tendency of most Irish-speaking parents to strive to ensure that their children could speak the 'modern' language, English.

While parental pressure and the ambition of the young themselves were undoubtedly the main forces in producing a precipitous decline in the use—and ultimately also the knowledge—of Gaelic, other major factors worked in the same direction. Although the Catholic Church was not opposed to the Irish language as such, few priests or bishops concerned themselves actively about its preservation: Archbishop John MacHale of Tuam was almost a solitary exception in the years 1830–45. In the negative sense at least, the weight of the Church's influence helped the spread of English. Much the same was true of mass constitutional politics during the O'Connell era. O'Connell, who spoke Irish fluently and used it occasionally in speeches and canvassing throughout his life, looked forward to the gradual decay of his native language with equanimity. In part, this was a reflection of the popular identification of Gaelic with backwardness, and in part an expression of his universal type of radicalism which sought to remove every apparent barrier to easy human communication and cooperation.

O'Connell was not immune to sentimental regret at the passing of his hereditary culture. But this counted for little with him compared with the business of Ireland's independence and advancement, which could, in his eyes, only be achieved by dealing with the British system on its own terms and in its own language. From the beginning of his agitation in 1808, and in particular from 1823 on, O'Connell's press and popular rallying campaigns were conducted almost entirely in English. As such, they were essentially if unintentionally inimical to the survival of Irish—and indeed to the traditional ways in general, despite his adoption of a 'native' kitsch of 'patriotic' symbols such as harps, round towers and wolfhounds.

A third force that subverted Gaelic was the Irish primary school system established in 1831. It was largely financed and practically controlled by the state, and the teaching in its schools was through English only. The 'national school' was a powerful engine in the spread of English and contributed significantly to the finding of the census of 1851 that only 5 per cent of the population was still monolingually Gaelic-speaking. Further, the new educational syllabus was Anglocentric in character as well as English in language. No Irish history or literature was taught; indeed, the only distinctively Irish element in the curriculum was the geography of the island. The cultural values to be inculcated were those that the ruling classes wished the work force to accept, such as respect for superiors and social docility; and the cultural frame of reference was exclusively British. The fact that both religious and national differentiations were ignored, if not positively discouraged, appears to have had no effect upon the pupils. Here home, parish and chapel were sufficient antidotes. But the gradual familiarisation with this alien social system and this other range of social and cultural criteria was probably an important preparation for living in communities dominated by Anglo-Saxon values, institutions, assumptions and modes of behaviour. Here, as with the use of English itself, was an important piece of 'baggage' for those pupils destined for later emigration—and it was probably the case that one out of three of the children being educated in the new national schools would lead his or her adult life overseas.

Increasing sectarianism

Not all the 'baggage' with which the Irish young were being equipped in the 1830s and 1840s would prove as useful to them in a new world as their Spartan upbringing, relative fluency in English and familiarity with British practices. These decades were also marked by a new intensity of religious and political asperity. Although the cause of Catholic emancipation had been supported by some Irish Protestants, once the *Relief Act* of 1829 was passed without (in

Protestant eyes) any apparent diminution in the Catholic 'threat' to their ultimate security, Irish politics became increasingly sectarian.

A major reason was that religion itself became more sectarian in certain ways. Since the 1790s the Irish Catholic Church had continued to grow not only in confidence but also in the numbers of its clergy, other religious parochial organisations, pious practices and charitable institutions; and during the second quarter of the nineteenth century it made a quantum leap forward in these respects. The proportion of priests who had been trained in European seminaries—in Spain, France, Portugal, the Low Countries and Rome—and generally reared in submissive and deferential attitudes to secular authority, was in decline. Contrariwise, Maynooth founded in 1795, and now the principal nursery for the parish clergy, had long thrown off such Gallican timidity and restraints. Moreover, European Catholicism in general was undergoing a sort of second Counter-Reformation, and Ireland shared fully in the new missionary zeal and even arrogance. How widely this extended throughout the country before 1845 is a matter of dispute among historians. The crux of the debate is the extent of regular church-going among those classified as Catholics. Despite various conflicts of evidence, this at least seems clear—that modern devotional practice and a new type of spiritual aggression seemed to march more or less in step with modernisation in general.

The Catholic developments were both matched and fuelled by Protestant equivalents. Irish Protestantism in all its forms was profoundly influenced by the Evangelical movement gathering strength in England since the late eighteenth century. Overall, this influence worked in Ireland in the direction of a more fundamentalist and 'vital' or emotional religion. The deepening fears of Roman Catholic pretensions at home reinforced the anti-sacramental, anti-sacerdotal and general anti-popery strains in Evangelicalism when it crossed the Irish Sea. In the Church of Ireland, this meant a growing dominance of Low Church doctrines and practices. In Presbyterianism, it led to a major schism as a stricter and harsher form of Calvinism gained the upper hand in that communion. Methodism and other dissenting sects, while remaining small in the numbers of their adherents, were reinvigorated and took the missionary offensive. In fact, all the Irish Protestant denominations, from about 1810 on, were touched to a greater or less degree by the proselytising spirit.

To Evangelicals of almost every stamp, the picture of the Irish peasantry as benighted victims of a tyrannical Romanism, awaiting rescue from darkness and damnation by the evangelists of true religion, was alluring. It had an especially powerful appeal in Britain where it was often accompanied by a corresponding vision of the Indian masses; and money and other resources for both missionary enterprises were forthcoming to a considerable extent in the first half of the nineteenth century. In Ireland, the main drive of the proselytising societies took place in the poorer and more seaward regions of the west and south-west because it was here (in the eyes of the enthusiasts) that the population was most 'backward'; least drilled in Roman Catholic errors, mummery and superstition; most under the thrall of traditional pagan practices; and least versed in the English language, and therefore least vulnerable to the new propaganda being brewed in Maynooth and the other seminaries.

Much of the Protestant missionary activity was conducted in Irish and based on Gaelic translations of the Bible. This in itself added to the political dimensions of the religious contest, as many Catholics were prone to outrage at the native tradition (which they themselves had done little or nothing to maintain) being 'turned against itself'. There were also charges that peasants in acute want were being bribed into Protestantism by food or other material advantages. 'Soupers', the very term popularly coined for the converts, was a jeering reference to the soup kitchens set up by some missions in times of famine or great want: it was the Irish equivalent of 'rice Christians'. Not all the direct tussle for souls, however, took place in the most distressed regions of Connacht and Munster. Especially during the late 1820s, a series of religious 'tournaments' between Protestant and Catholic polemicists took place, usually at Protestant instigation, in Dublin and other large centres of population. These often lasted several days and were widely attended and reported, although there is no evidence that the fiery disputations changed anybody's faith, at any rate immediately.

Protestants too had their reasons for calling 'foul play' in this sort of combat. Mixed marriages were regarded by them as a Roman ploy which would cost them the next generation, unless there was a pre-existing and honestly honoured agreement that male and female children should be reared, respectively, in the faith of the parent of the same sex. Nunneries were deeply suspected as a system of spiritual enslavement, in which even Protestant or would-be Protestant girls might be entrapped. The principal Protestant grievance of the 1820s was the succession of confrontations deliberately engineered by the Catholic Association. From the Association's standpoint, these were amply justified, first by the actual handicaps imposed on Catholics by the various manifestations of Protestant supremacy that were being assailed, and second by the great utility of agitating Catholic wrongs in drumming up support—especially clerical support—for its fundamental objective, emancipation. But to most Protestants they seemed a malignant conspiracy to upset the established social order. This view was confirmed for many when, after emancipation had been at last conceded, Catholic claims for equal treatment grew rapidly rather than abated. Such was the atmosphere in which most Irish Protestant emigrants to Australia (at least 20 per cent of the entire Irish emigration) were reared in the middle quarters of the nineteenth century.

Education reflected the same division. At the time of the Act of Union, the regular elementary and secondary school systems were both meagre and almost exclusively Protestant in character. Gradually, after 1800, a Catholic educational system run by religious orders developed. But it was very small in scale and largely confined to the cities and larger towns before 1845. It did embrace some of the children of the urban poor, but was outside the reach of the great majority, and scarcely touched the countryside at all. There the hedge schools still maintained some ground as educators of the rural middle class from place to place down to the Great Famine. They did not survive the calamity of 1845–52. In 1855 one witness testified to a Royal Commission:

> The famine nearly eliminated classical education [hedge schools]; and the better class of farmers who used to procure such education for their children has been broken down or has migrated. The smaller classical schools are nearly all gone.[7]

Meanwhile, the government was gradually drawn into the field of Catholic elementary education of a non-proselytising character. Education had begun to be regarded as an antidote to economic improvidence, violence and political disaffection. From 1815 to 1831 the state worked vicariously through the Kildare Place Society, a voluntary association professedly devoted to providing non-sectarian education for the poor. In practice it was, after 1820, generally condemned as sectarian by the Catholic leaders, lay and clerical alike. By 1831 there were, nonetheless, nearly 140 000 children in the system. In that year the state became directly involved in the matter by setting up a national education board to promote, control and, to a large extent, finance primary education. Within fifteen years the new system embraced over 4000 schools and nearly half a million pupils, even if attendances, being non-compulsory, were intermittent. Meanwhile, those who rejected this 'godless' form of education, in particular the Catholic bishops of the west under the leadership of John MacHale, and the great majority of the Anglican episcopate, had set up their own systems, catering for perhaps a further 150 000 children in 1845.

Fast as population and poverty were growing between the Act of Union and the famine, popular education was growing faster, especially from 1830 onward. One important effect was a dramatic fall in the national illiteracy rate. By 1841, it had dropped to 51, and by 1851 to 45 per cent, very impressive figures by contemporary European standards, especially in view of the composition and destitution of the Irish population. This did not necessarily mean real competency, let alone facility, in reading and writing: the standard set for 'literacy' was very low. But it did mean something—that over half the population, and in the younger age groups well over half the population, should have possessed at least the rudiments of the knowledge needed to function effectively in the modern world, and especially in the modern city and large town. The majority of Irish immigrants in Australia from the 1830s onwards were destined to settle ultimately in urban areas, and most were young enough to have been able to benefit—whether or not they had actually done so—from the Irish school reforms. Although their educational preparation was undoubtedly inferior to that of their English counterparts, it was far ahead of that of the preceding generations.

Management of Irish local government

The Irish day-to-day experience of government was also a useful preparation for colonial life. Even in the late eighteenth century, Ireland was remarkable for its administrative centralisation and degree of state intervention and support, not least in economic matters. In contrast to England, local government in Ireland was both small in scope and weak in action. Over most of the country, the ruling class was much too thinly spread and spent too little time on its estates for the English model of parish and shire self-management to work effectively. Moreover, there was little homogeneity of interest or sentiment between rulers and ruled in Ireland whereas the English system depended on a considerable measure of consensus for its success. Correspondingly, Ireland was too impoverished and commercially undeveloped for much business or manufacture to form itself 'spontaneously' in early capitalist fashion. In consequence of these factors, Irish government was decidedly more national and less regional than was the case in the larger and more stable and sophisticated kingdom.

In 1800, Ireland, with a population of approximately five million, was administered by twenty-two departments. No less than twelve of them were boards nominated by the government and some of these were composed of paid board members, in effect salaried officials. Several, such as the Linen Trust and the Internal Navigation Board, were devoted to industrial development or the provision of an economic infrastructure. During the first thirty years after the Act of Union, 1801–30, ten new statutory authorities were set up to deal with public health and welfare, as well as the customary economic development. In the following decade, 1831-40, when the Whigs were almost continuously in office, the process of state management of Ireland took on new dimensions. As we have seen, the first step was taken towards a universal system of primary education; the Board of Works was reorganised to become a country-wide agency for promoting economic growth; and a national police force, an Ecclesiastical Commission and a Poor Law Board, as well as a host of lesser statutory bodies, were instituted. Over the same period, the Irish public service was being transformed into a fully paid, professional and (in most cases) permanent corps. The appointment of people currently engaged in everyday politics was brought to an end.

All this was by no means as deliberately designed or as 'progressive' as it may look to twentieth-century eyes. Down to 1845, Ireland was for the most part growing poorer and more helpless (at least in comparison with Great Britain) with corresponding calls for more desperate and directive measures from on high. Meanwhile, the Irish pressures for political independence after 1830 were being answered at Westminster with attempts to buy off agitation through social and economic amelioration—an early form of 'killing Home Rule by kindness'. Similarly, the 'reformed' Irish civil service was still mainly recruited by patronage and favour. Down to the mid-1830s it was an exclusive Ascendancy preserve.

As the great nineteenth-century historian, W. E. H. Lecky, noted:

> In 1833, four years after Catholic emancipation, there was not in Ireland a single Catholic judge or stipendiary magistrate. All the high sheriffs, with one exception, the overwhelming majority of the unpaid magistrates and of the grand jurors, the five inspectors-general, and the thirty-two sub-inspectors of police, were Protestant.[8]

Despite some Catholic dilution thereafter, the Irish administration remained substantially Protestant in composition even up to the end of the nineteenth century; and Irish Protestantism was equated, generally justly, with loyalism, Ascendancy interests and the maintenance of the British connection. Again, many of the state undertakings failed, wholly or in part, because of poor planning, vested opposition or underfunding. Whatever the motivation or the outcome, however, a centralised form of positive and interventionist government had emerged in Ireland. British Cabinets in the first half of the nineteenth century had no hesitation in treating Ireland as:

> . . . a social laboratory. The most conventional of Englishmen were willing to experiment in Ireland on lines which they were not prepared to contemplate . . . at home.[9]

The *Constabulary Act* of 1836 and the reform of the Board of Works in 1831 are good examples of this statism. The first set up a single body of police responsible for order over the entire country, except for Dublin, Belfast and Derry; and even these city forces were coordinated with the rest. The essential novelties of the new Irish Constabulary were their complete centralisation and coordination, their professionalism and mobility, and their quasi-military organisation and discipline. These structures and features had been foreshadowed in the Peace Preservation force set up by Peel, as Irish Secretary, in 1814. The 1836 Acts, however, brought all Irish police under an ultimately united command, with an autonomous national inspectorate to enforce, as the original recommendation put it, 'one uniform system of rules and regulations for the entire Irish police establishment', and with a single, large training depot in Dublin to serve the entire force. Thus Ireland came to possess a coherent, stratified, paramilitary police at a time when the lonely, untrained village constable was still the instrument of law enforcement over most of rural England.

In the 1830s at least, police reform worked against the traditional Ascendancy. It so happened that, initially, it was state policy to treat the nationalist and popular movements with unwonted mildness, and their opposites with unwonted severity. This was not, to say the least of it, a permanent condition in Anglo–Irish relations; and in different circumstances the power and omnipresence of the Irish Constabulary assumed a very different mien in the eyes of the populace. Moreover, its mode of officer recruitment, on a caste basis like that of the armed services, was bound to lead, over time, to a considerable measure of identification between the bias of the constabulary and the interests of the gentry. But its work and significance were by no means exclusively political. Possibly the most important consequence of the police reforms was the provision of a modern underpinning for nineteenth-century Irish society. Agricultural statistics were collected, as well as political information; national censuses were handled, as well as the registration of firearms. It was not only political violence that was repressed: faction fighting and a host of other contemporary manifestations of brutality were slowly worn down.

A vast range of day-to-day duties, such as enforcing the current regulations governing slaughter-houses or weights and measures or poison schedules, imperceptibly established a new and more involved and responsible form of social organisation.

A similar situation occurred with the Board of Works as reconstituted in 1831. From 1817 onwards, the central government had provided grants for various public undertakings in Ireland, in itself an extraordinary departure given the contemporary British attitudes to state intervention. These undertakings extended from roads, bridges and harbours to areas such as fisheries and land drainage, which encroached, with compulsory powers of acquisition in some cases, upon private interests. There was even a distinct possibility, in the late 1830s, that Ireland would end up with a state-owned and state-managed railway system. Meanwhile, the Board's inspectors were led on by Irish exigencies into general economic planning and even an attempt to determine a wages policy.

The new Board of Works had spent just over a million pounds in grants as well as loans by 1845. Even though this sum was trivial in terms of Irish need, not merely was the Board being geared, unwittingly, for the impending crisis of the Great Famine, but also it was foreshadowing a new form and philosophy of government—indeed, a revolutionary view of society. In time the inspectors developed their own expertise, and the largeness of their task drew them into ever more distant fields. The railway commission had been as much concerned with providing employment as with providing transport. The debate on drainage largely centred on the issue of land resources. The ideas that the building of an economic infrastructure was the state's responsibility, that the economy should be continually primed and steered, and that the critical decisions should come from experts and from above, were all unfolding here. A new sort of policy was being prefigured.

Much the same could be said of the Australian colonies in the earlier decades of white settlement. For a variety of reasons, from the regulated character of the original establishment to the want of initial capital, and from the problems of building an infrastructure quickly to the paucity of a gentry, colonial government resembled the Irish administration much more closely than it did the British. In fact, if the Hiberno–Westminster and Australian–Westminster systems of the early nineteenth century are compared, several striking similarities seem evident. There were of course also fundamental differences arising from, *inter alia*, the common parliamentary and (in certain fields) administrative institutions of Great Britain and Ireland, and the internal and gradually effective Irish opposition to the Act of Union. None the less, in the weakness of local government; in the initiating and managerial role of the state; in the degree of public control and the comparatively large and powerful bureaucracies that were its accompaniment; and in the authoritarian and collectivist flavours of the regimes, the systems show remarkable resemblances.

It would not be difficult to find reasons why two such apparently diverse areas of rule should have developed in similar directions in many fields. To put it at its very simplest, both were dependencies with acute problems of public order. Correspondingly, it would be interesting to establish the degree to which Ireland provided actual precedents or models for the Australian colonies in their institutional infancy. Even in our present meagre state of knowledge, we can point to direct influences of prime importance. The colonial police forces, for example, were formed on the pattern of the Irish Constabulary of 1836 and drew many of their first officers from that body. Especially important, as Mark Finnane points out, was the repetition of the 'centralised, bureaucratically organised'[10] Irish principles. Similarly, the Irish national school system of 1831 was the forerunner of the state school systems of the Australian colonies, which continued to call on the Irish

National Board of Education for occasional advice. The list of derivations or inspirations may be considerably extended as various new fields of early Australian government are explored. If so, it should cause no surprise. The Irish pressures usually predated the Australian; and if necessity were the mother of invention, it was perhaps only to be expected that Ireland would make first call upon her services.

Meanwhile, Irish immigrants in the southern colonies would have found the governmental ethos of their new home remarkably familiar.

4

The Age of O'Connell: 1830–50

1830–45

The years 1830–45 constitute a particularly interesting epoch. Looking back, we inevitably see this decade and a half as a prelude to the tragic and tremendous watershed of the Great Famine. But although a few spoke vaguely of some pending catastrophe, as the gap between resources and population ever widened, no contemporary could really envisage the disaster that lay ahead. So, we must make the effort to repress our after-knowledge if we are to understand what moved people at the time, just as we should have to do if, say, we were trying to recover the 'felt' reality of France in 1773–88, the decade and a half immediately preceding the Revolution. In this light, the comparative hopefulness often manifest in Ireland in the pre-famine years becomes more comprehensible. A large and growing population was then commonly taken to constitute national strength; and poverty, in such a case as Ireland's, could be easily represented as the necessary consequence of alien domination.

This leads on to a second important feature of the epoch. It was marked by a powerful rising wave of Irish nationalism in which the Act of Union was denounced as the fountain of all Ireland's miseries and the murderer of Irish prosperity.

It was a simplistic and absolutist creed. All evils tended to be attributed to a single, clearly discernible cause, and the remedy for all was held to be implicit in the repeal of a single parliamentary measure.

The Agitator-General

From the very outset of his public career in 1800, O'Connell spoke of the repeal of the Act of Union as his ultimate political objective. Through all the years of Catholic campaigning, he steadily maintained that emancipation was but the preliminary (though also necessary) step towards this final end. He always asked, literally, for the restoration of the Irish Parliament of the late eighteenth century; but he cannot have supposed, when he began to agitate in earnest for it in 1830, that this was either possible or in the Catholic interest. What he really sought was to force Britain to the bargaining table and then extract from her the utmost constitutional concession. But a demagogue needs slogans not hypothetical complexity; and the call to destroy a supposed infamy by one simple stroke answered his purpose well.

Although O'Connell's was a career of endless manoeuvres and judicious confusion both his political purposes and his political philosophy were remarkably unchanging from first to last. This philosophy centred around three major propositions, derived from the utopian radicalism of the 1790s, the years of his early manhood: first, that in terms of civil right all persons, irrespective of race, colour or religion, were free and equal; second, that the use of violence to achieve a political end was counter-productive as well as morally wrong; and third that every desirable reform could sooner or later be achieved by educating and mobilising the concentrated force of public opinion. Despite multitudinous pressures and innumerable crises, O'Connell adhered substantially to these general principles throughout his public life. Even more, given all the difficulties of the circumstances, he imposed them to an extraordinary degree upon his followers.

He first raised the banner of repeal, and set up the first of his many repeal organisations, in 1830, when at last (at the age of 55) he entered the House of Commons. The banner was immediately lowered because the issue of parliamentary reform began to dominate British politics from the moment of his entry. As an advanced radical, O'Connell felt that he must concentrate his energies immediately on supporting the reform cause. Like emancipation, parliamentary reform seemed—or could plausibly be presented as—a necessary preliminary to repeal. When the *Reform Act* was finally on the statute books in 1832 (with almost no direct advantage to Ireland), O'Connell raised his banner once more at the subsequent general election, and attempted to build up an Irish party pledged to struggle for repeal.

To some extent, he succeeded. Nearly forty MPs more or less committed to repeal (one cannot be more precise because of uncertainties as to the degree of commitment) and a smaller number more or less committed to O'Connell's general leadership were returned at the election. Despite the emphasis on winning Irish seats on the issue of repeal, O'Connell had no desire to bring the matter before the House of Commons immediately. He was fully aware that he would be opposed by almost every British member of the House, as well as by the remaining sixty-five Irish MPs, and end up defeated by the crushing margin of 20 or 25 to 1 against. But he could not keep repeal off-stage for long, as a sort of weapon that might be used if other Irish needs remained unmet. Not only had he already stirred up opinion at home upon the issue but also his would-be rival as popular leader, Feargus O'Connor (destined later to head the Chartist movement), forced his hand by threatening to introduce a pro-repeal motion in the House of Commons at once should O'Connell continue to drag his feet. By various devices, O'Connell delayed the motion for as long as possible, but when at last, in April 1834, the fatal debate came on, the outcome was precisely what he had feared—utter rejection of the proposal and a humiliating exposure of the futility of pleading the repeal cause as a simple issue in the British Parliament.

Meanwhile, during 1830–34 O'Connell had used his front-line standing in the House of Commons both to criticise British rule in Ireland systematically and to press for various, mostly minor Irish reforms. With the Whig–Liberals under Earl Grey in government, and dependent on O'Connell's support for their Reform Bill, his position should have been comparatively strong; and in fact a few conciliatory measures in fields such as education and Church of Ireland 'temporalities' (clerical income) were carried through. But the government could rely on solid Tory support in all its efforts to crush O'Connell's associations and agitations in Ireland; and on this point it remained his unbending enemy before it split up in mid-1834 on the issue of how far it should yield to his pressures for further inroads on the Church of Ireland.

When, after a brief Tory interlude, the Whig–Liberals (having shed Grey and their most right-wing element) resumed power in April 1835, their relationship with O'Connell was very different. The intervening general election held in January had left them dependent on his support for office. By the so-called Lichfield House Compact, an unwritten and in part tacit agreement, the two parties came to terms. O'Connell 'contracted' to throw the thirty or so votes he still controlled in the House of Commons on the side of Lord Melbourne's ministry, and also to suspend the repeal and other active agitations, in return for a share in the nomination of new Irish appointments to government offices and honours, and a series of Irish remedial measures ranging from the abolition of the tithes paid to the Church of Ireland to municipal and local government reform. The Whigs were therefore to be secured in government by O'Connell's parliamentary backing, and given a relatively easy passage in Ireland through O'Connell's pacificatory and conciliatory influence. Correspondingly, his role at home was not unlike that of a paramount chief. The whole arrangement might almost be described as a species of indirect rule.

The Lichfield House Compact was a gentlemen's agreement, and politicians as politicians are rarely gentlemen. There were many infringements of the understanding even before it withered in the last two years of Melbourne's ministry, 1839–41. The Whigs could plead, with some justice, that their bills had to be pared down, sometimes reduced to near-shadows, if they were to pass a fiercely hostile House of Lords, with an entrenched Conservative majority. O'Connell could plead, with some justice, that he was a popular leader who had to pay constant attention to the voices of the led, on whom he depended not merely for his political power but also for his very income and standing in the world. He could not afford to appear too accommodating to a British government. He needed palpable concessions and favours to justify his muted opposition.

Given all this, the quasi-alliance between the Whig cabinet and the O'Connellites in Parliament worked tolerably well for approximately four years, even if the end of Lord Melbourne's administration was marked by mutual disenchantment and ill-feeling. In legislative terms, the harvest was meagre from O'Connell's point of view. 'Reforms' were achieved in most of the designated areas. They were, however, usually reduced to very little in the course of their storm-tossed passage through the House of Lords. The *Grand Jury Act* (1837) produced a slightly more responsible and coherent form of county government but left power, virtually intact, in landlord hands. Tithes were ostensibly abolished in 1838 but their burden on the tenants was not really removed; instead it was transferred in large part to rents. A Poor Law was introduced in Ireland in 1840, but this consisted of a crude imposition of the inappropriate English model, in the teeth of all Irish experience and advice. It barely touched the fringes of the problem of Irish

70

poverty and was quickly overwhelmed once the Great Famine struck. The *Municipal Reform Act* (1840) popularised urban government to a degree and effectively opened it up to Catholic participation, but only at the cost of emasculating the powers of corporations and reducing their number to thirteen.

Not all the Irish reforming legislation of 1835–41 was as limited in effect as the major measures; but even the most mutilated statutes advanced the nationalist cause in some degree. The *Municipal Reform Act*, for example, broke the exclusive hold of Protestant Unionists on city government, even if their Catholic supplanters entered into a much diminished inheritance. Moreover, as with emancipation, there were the important psychic satisfactions to be taken into account. On each front, the Ascendancy had been forced to yield a certain amount of ground, after a protracted struggle in which the anomalies in their situation had been thoroughly exposed. Although the 'retreats' were partly illusory, every apparently backward step by the Irish Tories cheered their assailants, and infused them with the feeling that history was on their side.

Of at least equal significance was the conduct of Irish government and the distribution of Irish patronage during the later 1830s. Down to 1834 Dublin Castle had conducted its affairs on an unabashedly partisan basis. It was manned almost exclusively by right-wing Protestants, and distributed both its brickbats and its bouquets in the interest of that faction. This was anathema to O'Connell. A major, if not indeed the central, drive of his manoeuvres in the 1830s was to achieve a degree (as high as possible, of course) of power-sharing in Ireland.

He was remarkably successful in his pursuit of this objective during the earlier years of Melbourne's administration. First, the key position of Irish undersecretary was held by Thomas Drummond, a Scot and former officer in the Royal Engineers who had taken part in the Irish Ordnance Survey during the preceding decade. Drummond

71

determined on even-handed government in Ireland, to replace the customary steady bias in favour of Orangeism and the Protestant Ascendancy. Not quite without cause, he was even accused of favouring the Catholic faction on occasions. So far as he succeeded, it seemed a world turned upside down to all the Irish protagonists.

A key element in Drummond's efforts to provide disinterested rule was the newly formed Irish Constabulary (later, the Royal Irish Constabulary) which was instructed, generally effectively, to provide impartial enforcement of the law. That he could count on an obedient police force was largely to the credit of two Peninsular War veterans, General Shaw Kennedy and Colonel McGregor, who had reordered and freshly disciplined the body. He could also count on another new instrument of government, paid resident magistrates, to carry out his policy. Several of these men, too, were former serving soldiers who were accustomed to executing orders, whether palatable or unpalatable. Like the others, they tended to see themselves as olympians, well above the petty quarrels of the natives whom they had been called upon to rule. The phenomenon is one familiar in the earlier decades of Australian colonial history, when much of the administration was placed in the hands of retired or half-pay British military or naval officers.

Similarly, the hold of the Ascendancy on government patronage was well and truly, if only temporarily, broken. From 1835 on, the bulk of the offices, distinctions and largesse at the disposal of the ministry went to Irish liberals, whether Protestant or Catholic. Most of the beneficiaries were in fact drawn from the sparse ranks of Liberal Protestants. This was not surprising. The majority of the posts and other appointments demanded either professional qualifications or a social and financial standing that, as yet, comparatively few Catholics had attained. O'Connell himself was far from opposed to Protestants being chosen. On the contrary, he was eager to establish that Irish nationalism was thoroughly non-sectarian in character; a very moderate degree of sympathy for national and liberal ends sufficed for him to support a Protestant aspirant. Nevertheless, a not inconsiderable number of Catholics were appointed to the judiciary and magistracy, as well as to offices (some of them sinecures or near-sinecures) under the Crown.

Again, this seemed to Irish Tories a stunning role reversal. It was surely against all nature, against the merest prudence, that 'disloyal' Papists and their Protestant fellow-travellers should be infiltrated into the Irish power-base. The old guard in Dublin Castle and the Ascendancy in general were determined to reverse the process once the Whig–Liberals were driven out of office. So they did, to some extent, when the Conservatives returned to power in 1841. But a vital precedent had been set. The door once opened could never be completely closed. Indeed, not only had a nexus been established between Liberal governments and a Roman Catholic share of Irish appointments, but also Peel and the Conservative leadership were determined to detach the Catholic Church, so far as possible, from O'Connell's movements even if this meant 'sacrificing' some of the positions and honours that would otherwise go to Irish ultra-Protestants. The change in Tory tactics was clearly apparent in 1843–45.

The Repeal Association

As early as 1838 O'Connell made threatening motions as well as noises, on the subject of repeal; but these did not result in any real break with the Whigs until 1840. Even then, when he set up the Repeal Association, he did little to press home his attack. He still had not escaped completely from the thrall of the Whig–Liberal alliance. The general election of 1841, however, made it all too clear that the alliance was buried as well as dead. Not only was there no union of forces in the Irish constituencies but also the Whig–Liberals went out of their way to repudiate any association with O'Connell when the new Parliament assembled. Peel's Conservative Party had now a secure overall majority and the number of O'Connellite MPs had been much reduced, from lack of both money and zeal in the conduct of the campaign. O'Connell himself seemed an exhausted force, wearied out by nearly forty years of strenuous and often feverish political activity and excitement. Over the past three years, he had talked or written several times about retirement, even to contemplating permanent retreat to some monastery!

O'Connell had despaired prematurely. The new *Municipal Reform Act* provided him fortuitously with an opening: he saw that he could now win the Lord Mayorship of Dublin. Suddenly, in the autumn of 1841, he threw himself into the work of creating an urban political machine in the city wards. All his old organisational gifts, honourable and otherwise, sprang instantly into play. He created a political juggernaut out of nothing, and reduced the long-reigning Orange party to a small and impotent minority. To the world outside, it was a petty triumph, a lordship of Lilliput. To O'Connell it was an opportunity for both personal and public rehabilitation and display, and a mode of demonstrating to near and far the magnanimity and governmental capacity of the native Irish. During his year as Lord Mayor, 1841–42, he largely neglected the House of Commons and concentrated on projecting an image of non-partisan administration, managerial efficiency, rectitude and popular pomp and majesty. In his own eyes and those of his followers, at least, his 'rule' was an object lesson of the nationalist capacity for self-government.

Restored and rekindled, O'Connell threw himself into a thorough reconstruction of the Repeal Association as soon as he left office in October 1842. Although he was by now in his sixty-eighth year, he had recovered all his old energy and spirit. Westminster was totally forsaken. Instead, Ireland was to be the battlefield, and agitation on a scale hitherto undreamt of, his mode of war. The revived Association was highly centralised, with O'Connell himself as the commanding figure. He dominated both his 'cabinet' of subordinates and every national committee. None the less, local organisation based on the parish unit and generally under the chairmanship of the parish clergy provided the movement's motive force. This was because O'Connell sought to weld nationalist Ireland into a huge though single instrument of pressure. Religious structures and the priests were indispensable in mobilising the rural millions.

He began by declaring that 1843 would be the repeal year, a promise that the Act of Union would be repealed before its close. Even in his most euphoric moments, he can scarcely have believed that this would happen. It is much more likely that his initial declaration was meant as an opening gambit in a struggle to achieve some significant degree of Irish constitutional independence. In certain respects, he succeeded beyond his most daring hope. The 'Monster Meetings'—popular assemblages in strategic centres all about the country—were the centrepiece of the campaign. Nearly forty of them were held during 1843 mostly on Sundays, with O'Connell himself usually the star. They were elaborately—not to add, histrionically—staged, and demanded miracles of planning and preparation. Thousands of stewards and 'repeal police' were required for crowd control and program management, especially as the numbers mounted during the summer and early autumn of the year.

In certain respects, the monster meetings were people's festivals, though marked by sobriety and regimentation rather than licence. Perhaps the most striking, in terms of size and discipline at least, was the great demonstration on the Hill of Tara, Co. Meath, on 'Lady Day', 15 August 1843. The lowest published reckoning of the numbers present was 800 000; certainly, the total must have exceeded half a million. The celebrated English author, Bulwer Lytton, who was present, described in memorable verse O'Connell's matchless power of voice and command of a mass audience:

> Walled by wide air and roofed by boundless heaven;
> Beneath his feet the human ocean lay,

And wave on wave flowed into space away.
Methought no clarion could have sent its sound
E'en to the centre of the hosts around.
And, as I thought, rose a sonorous swell,
As from some church tower swings the silvery bell;
Aloft and clear from airy tide to tide,
It glided easy as a bird may glide.
To the last verge of that vast audience sent,
It played with each wild passion as it went:
Now stirred the uproar, now the murmurs stilled,
And sobs or laughter answered as it willed.
Then did I know what spell of infinite choice
To rouse or lull has the sweet human voice
Then did I learn to seize the sudden clue
To the grand troublous life-antique to view,
Under the rock-stand of Demosthenes,
Unstable Athens heave her noisy seas.

The Monster Meetings were designed with three main ends in view. The first was to show the magnitude of the support for repeal. The assemblages were huge in scale; that at the Hill of Tara on 15 August was, as we have seen, at least half a million or thereabouts in number. The second was to show that it represented almost the entire nation. The meetings were so distributed that no part of the country (the Protestant north-east corner excepted) was more than twenty-five miles (40 km) from one or other of the meeting locations; and everywhere the attendances were very large. The third objective was to demonstrate O'Connell's absolute command of these vast masses. On his instructions, the crowds were altogether sober, orderly and peaceful. O'Connell boasted later that in an entire year of fervid and massive agitation not a single person had suffered any bodily injury. The other side of the coin was that O'Connell held this tremendous force in hand. Should his grip weaken or be released, incalculable popular violence might be unrestrainable. Such at least was his implicit threat.

Peel's government was in a dilemma. By now it was conventional wisdom in British Conservative circles that O'Connell was a spent force, whose hold over the Irish people had been broken well before his relatively weak showing in the general election of 1841. For most of 1843 the government adhered to the line that the repeal agitation was a sham, an attempted confidence trick by a discredited political swindler. To make any move against O'Connell would be to play into his hands, endowing his latest venture with an importance to which it had no intrinsic claim. By the time that such truly Monster Meetings as that of Tara were being held, however, the Cabinet began to feel alarmed. Behind the scenes, Peel and his chief lieutenant, Sir James Graham, sought to devise 'non-political' Irish reforms which (it was supposed) would cut the ground from under O'Connell's feet. These were to be supplemented by religious concessions that might detach the more conservative elements in the Catholic Church from the repeal movement. At the same time, the government must avoid all appearance of yielding to O'Connell. Hence the decision to suppress the Association if a suitable legal pretext could be found.

A pretext was eventually found just before the final Monster Meeting of the year, to be held at Clontarf, near Dublin, early in October. The crowds were already moving in from the countryside when the meeting was declared illegal, with O'Connell commanding, and securing, total submission to this draconian decree, lest Ireland be plunged into bloodshed. Simultaneously, Dublin Castle ordered his arrest and the arrests of his principal subordinates on charges of sedition. Eight months later, they were found guilty by a Tory Dublin jury, and sentenced to imprisonment in Richmond Gaol. The arrests and sentences saved the great agitation of 1843 from a banal conclusion: some time before O'Connell had prudently withdrawn his threat to end the year with 'elections' to a national assembly, a quasi-parliament of his own. He also turned his 'martyrdom' at

Richmond to excellent political account through his publicity machines; and his release in August 1844, when the House of Lords upheld his appeal against the verdict, produced a climax of triumph and adulation far exceeding any that even he had experienced before.

The long campaign had won important hidden gains for O'Connell's cause. First, it had forced the government to abandon its contemptuous attitude towards repeal. In the end, it had brutally employed the state's coercive powers against a movement that it had hitherto dismissed as negligible. Next, it had driven Peel and Graham into moderating their support of ultra-Protestantism in Ireland, and instead to attempting to woo conservative Irish Catholics, clerical and lay alike, by a few conciliatory moves and a small share in the fruits of patronage. Finally, it had induced the Tory Cabinet, and especially Graham, to take up the consideration, at least, of a program of Irish land and other economic reforms to draw off some of the pressure that had been tapped by O'Connell throughout 1843. This policy departure was to have very significant consequences in the longer run. Thus, those who write off the great repeal campaign as an unadulterated failure are quite mistaken.

However, it would be foolish to deny that O'Connell had suffered a grievous defeat. First and foremost, the government had suppressed his movement and humiliated him without so much as one Irish fist being raised in outrage. O'Connell's principal concern had always been that his order against all forms of violence should be obeyed. This may have been consistent with his preaching from first to last, but the *demonstration* that no physical resistance need be feared robbed him of his most powerful weapon in dealing with British statesmen. Second, the weary months of imprisonment, on top of the titanic physical, oratorial and organisational exertions of 1843, demoralised O'Connell. Despite an ebullient first appearance after his release from Richmond, he emerged a half-broken man, determined only that he should never again conduct a protracted campaign or risk incarceration. Third, he had lost the aura of invincibility, of an inexorable political advance, which the 1843 agitation had engendered; and with this his support began to crumble here and there.

Among the defectors were several members of the Catholic episcopate and higher clergy who had always been alarmed by O'Connell's popular power. During 1844 Peel was able to draw these off by measures favourable to the further Catholic claims. More diffusely—and at the opposite end of the scale—O'Connell's tame acceptance of the prohibition of the Clontarf meeting, and his persistent later calls for obedience to the law and continued loyalty to the Crown, eroded his support among the more ardent and self-sufficient repealers. Gradually, his ultra-caution nauseated them and began to smack of timorousness and servility. It seemed increasingly evident that it was a price being paid for very little. At any rate, it would not buy the goods being sought. It was at this point that the movement later to be called Young Ireland came into being.

The birth of Young Ireland

Young Ireland is much to the fore in conventional Irish–Australian history; and it is very natural that this should be so. The Young Irelanders transported to Van Diemen's Land were extraordinarily gifted and colourful, as well as already famous or notorious, people. More, they were highly articulate people, well accustomed to advertising their wrongs and ambitions in fine and ringing prose and speeches and facile verse. Their comparatively short sojourn in Van Diemen's Land produced dramatic escapes and controversies over words of honour, and made its own interesting contribution to the folklore as well as the history of the island. While they stayed, they continued to draw some measure of international attention to their 'prison'. They left behind tourist 'shrines' such as William Smith O'Brien's cottage at

*The centenary of Daniel O'Connell's birth on 6 August 1775
was widely and variously celebrated throughout the colonies.
It did not lead, as was the case in Ireland, to bitter internal
conflicts between different factions of Irish nationalism.*

Port Arthur or the pathetic tombstone at Richmond marking the grave of Thomas Francis Meagher's infant son.

Yet, although the effect of the Young Irelanders on the course of Australian development was far more than episodic and legendary, it cannot compare in importance with the effect of O'Connellism, ill-recognised though that may be. It was O'Connell who drew the Catholic Church into active politics and gave the priests and bishops crucial roles in his campaigns and organisations. Later the clerical appetite grew with feeding: many of the clergy acquired a taste for independent political action and attempted to exercise influence. All this was of course muted in the Australian colonies, where demography, geography, the secular spirit and comparatively democratic institutions and liberal habits all worked against the tight controls and necessity for clear local leadership that were evident in nineteenth century Ireland. Nevertheless, the Church was, intermittently at least, a very significant factor in Australian politics from the 1840s onwards, and in this it bore many of the marks of original O'Connellism.

Much more important, however, was the virtual invention by O'Connell of many of the modes and mechanisms of modern mass politics, and their subsequent transference to Australia. O'Connell's organisational forms and ideological methods did not spring fully shaped from his creative imagination. Rather were they the product of long and painful trial and error, though all the more effective for being hammered out through hard experience. Taken together, they constituted an almost complete armoury for constitutional democratic action—in persuasion and propaganda, in the field, at the hustings, at the polls and ultimately in parliament itself. Between 1805 and 1845 many thousands of Irishmen had formed part, for some time, of one or other of O'Connell's political machines; and of these a due proportion became Australian immigrants in the course of time. From Roger Therry and John Henry Plunkett through John O'Shanassy to Charles Gavan Duffy, a line of leading colonial politicians had been first trained in O'Connell's 'school'. But there were many hundreds of lesser party workers and local organisers who had received the same political education, and applied it similarly to their new situations. Over and above the Irish themselves, the emergent colonial representative systems were deeply influenced by O'Connell's pioneering work in the focusing of public pressures upon governments and in a host of other features of the coming democratic order. The effect of all this on nineteenth century and later Australian politics may be incalculable, but was, and is, unquestionably immense.

Revolutionary nationalism

The revival of revolutionist nationalism in the later 1840s had little immediate connection with the United Irish tradition. It was a gradual development rather than a simple resurrection. The first, and in many ways foremost, factor was the establishment in October 1842, under the editorship of, among others, Charles Gavan Duffy, of the *Nation* newspaper. It was instantly successful. Its circulation was, by contemporary standards, extraordinarily large; and its outer clientele—those who borrowed copies, those who perused it in Repeal Reading Rooms and, above all, those to whom it was read aloud—was also on a quite unprecedented scale. Moreover, a considerable component of the *Nation*'s readership was the new class of well-educated young Catholics and a fair proportion of their Protestant counterparts. This provided O'Connell with a fresh body of zealous and idealistic propagandists and party workers. They supplied much dynamism, but also in the long run a serious challenge to his movement.

At first, the *Nation* group (more commonly called, after 1846, Young Ireland) appeared to present no danger to O'Connell. His prestige was still immense, and 'repeal' was an open-ended objective, capable of embracing almost all types and degrees of Irish nationalism. There were, however, hidden antagonisms even from the start between the old and the new elements in the Association. O'Connell's concept of independence was essentially constitutional and formal. For him, the subjective sense of nationality was not an issue. For him, Irish distinctiveness was a self-evident proposition, as well as delineated by nature itself in the island shape. Correspondingly, Irish independence did not mean total separation from Great Britain but rather that Ireland should be, as nearly as practicalities allowed, the equal of England, in role and status, within the continuing larger entity of the Empire, which was after all an Irish as well as a British construct. Thus political and civil parity, without necessarily changing the social and economic orders significantly, was O'Connell's final goal.

Contrariwise, the nationalism of Thomas Davis, the originating genius and inspiration of the *Nation* group, was essentially subjective, cultural and separatist in emphasis; it was also deeply influenced by what the late twentieth century would call the search for identity. For Davis, independence meant idiosyncrasy and difference—a quite distinctive way of life, set of attitudes and values, political system and, if possible, language, literature and art. If, in the midst of the tumultuous repeal movement, he never specifically endorsed Wolfe Tone's dictum, 'Break the connexion with England', it certainly expressed his inmost drive—and that in wider senses than Tone himself (who regarded Gaelic civilisation as merely primitive) had ever dreamt of. A sojourn in Germany after his graduation from Dublin University had left Davis enamoured of romantic nationalism of the German, and more specifically the Prussian, type. The consequent emphasis upon national history and national glory was, inevitably, militaristic.

This implicit challenge to the peaceful constitutional methods of agitation imposed by O'Connell upon the repeal movement was not initially apparent. Even O'Connell himself might have safely and happily endorsed the *Nation's* favourite Irish feats of arms—those against the Tudor forces of the sixteenth century, the Parliamentary, Cromwellian and Williamite armies of the seventeenth and (as the Irish Brigade) the anti-French coalitions of 1700–50. These were all, in rosy retrospect, chivalrous and heroic ventures; they were also usefully remote in time. There were other elements, however, in the new propaganda that were decidedly at odds with the spirit of O'Connellism. The constant 'flash of pike and sword' in the Young Ireland ballads—not to mention the fact that they were composed as 'marching songs'—inevitably instilled an admiration for revolutionary violence, especially in schoolboy and adolescent breasts.

The cumulative effect of years of such indoctrination was to change the disposition of large numbers in the coming generation. John O'Leary later recalled the *Nation*'s impact upon the schoolboys of the mid-1840s:

> In leading article, essay, and poem we read, from week to week, the story of Ireland's sufferings under English rule; and now and then we heard of other countries groaning under alien domination, and of their efforts, successful or unsuccessful, to shake it off. At first, perhaps, the teaching of the *Nation* was not directly unconstitutional, though, indirectly, it certainly was so from the beginning. From ceasing to 'fear to speak of '98' to wishing to imitate the men of that time the transition was very easy indeed to the youthful mind. Many, if not most, of the younger amongst us were Mitchelites before Mitchel, or rather before Mitchel had put forth his program.[11]

The tension between O'Connellism and Davisism remained below the surface, however, until after O'Connell's release from Richmond and subsequent abstention from agitation. When it did manifest itself in 1845, the basis was sectarian, Davis having an almost neurotic suspicion of popery and of O'Connell's close relations with his episcopal and other clerical allies—as well as an instinctive distaste for O'Connell's type of machine politics. But the more fundamental ideological divergence emerged only after Davis's death later in the same year. Having tacitly but permanently abandoned mass agitation, O'Connell now rested his hopes once again on the parliamentary method and a Liberal alliance—the Tories would shortly lose office on the Corn Law issue. Conversely, the Davisites began to toy with the notion of armed resistance to British rule in Ireland, and a return to the revolutionary tradition. In fact, Davis's successor as editor of the *Nation*, John Mitchel, an intransigent Ulster Presbyterian, was clearly bent on advocating violent courses almost from the start.

By mid-1846, O'Connell was determined to rid his movement of his Young Ireland critics, partly because their militaristic language placed the Repeal Association in legal danger, and partly to facilitate cooperation with the Whig–Liberals when they regained government. He was also, by now, ageing rapidly, in the grip of his final illness, and beyond the limit of his patience with the repeated challenges to his authority by young men forty or even more years his junior. Accordingly, he forced the issue by proposing that the specific repudiation of all forms of physical force in the pursuit of political ends be a condition of membership of the Repeal Association. After various ins-and-outs, O'Connell's ultimatum led to the withdrawal of the Young Ireland faction *en bloc*, with William Smith O'Brien literally as well as figuratively at their head.

The full implications of this division in Irish nationalism were far from apparent immediately. During the short remainder of his life, O'Connell devoted comparatively little attention to his domestic foes. He was increasingly absorbed in improving and exploiting his relations with the new Whig–Liberal government of Lord John Russell and, still more, in attempting to grapple with the fearful social and economic consequences of the Great Famine. Smith O'Brien, although *de facto* commander of the dissidents, provided little leadership at first, and the Irish Confederation (the Young Irelanders' formal organisation) was not even instituted until early in 1847. It seems to have had nothing more than propagandist aims in view at the beginning.

O'Connell's 'victory' was, however, a hollow thing. He was no longer capable of vigorous control of a national movement. Indeed, his health soon quite broke down, and on 15 May 1847 he died in Genoa in the course of a sad and futile 'pilgrimage' to Rome. His third son, John, whom he had designated his political heir, failed utterly to measure up to the succession. This break was the first great spur to the new Confederation. The second was the 'February Revolution' of 1848 in Paris which set off a chain of demonstrations-turned-insurrections and tottering thrones across the face of Continental Europe.

Young Ireland's legacy

The Irish Confederation failed to capitalise on the opportunities offered it during 1847 by John O'Connell's fumbling and ineptitude, by the deepening social crisis in most of Ireland, and by the lack of an effective response to it by the Whig government. It made some headway in the cities and larger towns, especially in Dublin, and among the intelligentsia, professional classes and artisans. But it lacked almost any support in the countryside, partly because the great majority of the priests were deeply antagonistic to the movement, and partly because the Confederation was driven by Smith O'Brien and Gavan Duffy to woo the landlords rather than the masses. The most potent voice to be raised against them within the Young Ireland movement was that of James Fintan Lalor: or so at least it sounds in posterity's ear.

Lalor rejected conventional politics and focused attention on the land which he held to belong collectively to the Irish people. Within the limits of the existing social system, he demanded, as a minimum, affordable rents and guaranteed security of tenure. Further, he proposed a strategy: immediate 'moral insurrection', by which he meant a national refusal to pay rents until both the British government and the Irish landlords conceded a new agricultural order that would allow tenants an assured and tolerable standard of life. Very few Young Irelanders accepted Lalor's proposed change of front, although Mitchel, who had little sympathy with his doctrine, was much attracted by the confrontation, class conflict and probable use of physical force implicit in a so-called moral insurrection. But Lalor was a harbinger of the future. In many ways, he foreshadowed the major concerns of Irish history in the second half of the nineteenth century.

Correspondingly, the February Revolution of 1848 in Paris opened up new vistas for Young Ireland. The lesson from the Continent seemed to be that governments could be overthrown by popular demand and demonstrations, with little or no bloodshed. But it was the British Cabinet rather than Young Ireland that produced a specific plan of action in response to the Continental precedent. Mitchel was the first victim of a new *Irish Coercion Act* rushed through Parliament. He was sentenced to transportation to Van Diemen's Land for sedition in June 1848. Meanwhile the Young Ireland command—if indeed there was any system of authority other than Smith O'Brien's pre-eminence in the movement—had talked and written themselves into a situation where an armed uprising seemed inescapable. When it actually came about, in July 1848, lack of prior planning or preparation, and the want of both leadership and strategic objectives, rendered it a near-fiasco, although also a near-bloodless fiasco. The battle of the Widow McCormack's cabbage plot, as the scoffers termed it, made it easy for the British press to hold up the Irish revolutionary movement to ridicule. But it also created an embarrassment for the British government. Four of the main participants in the attempted outbreak, Smith O'Brien, T. F. Meagher, T. B. McManus and Patrick O'Donoghue, having been found guilty of high treason, were automatically subject to the death sentence. The folly of making martyrs for no good reason was obvious even to Dublin Castle. The condemned men caused consternation by refusing to apply for pardons, and would by law have had to have been executed, if the government had not rushed through special legislation allowing the death sentence to be commuted to transportation, even without appeal.

The Young Irelanders rose rapidly to a moderate degree of martyrdom in the popular Irish estimation. This was true not only of the transportees and their counterparts who had fled to the United States or France but also of the scores of lesser figures who sought refuge abroad, and even of those at home too insignificant in the movement to warrant official notice. By no means did all of these remain committed revolutionists, or even sympathisers with the cause of violence. In fact, none of the four eventually transported for high treason—to take but a single instance—was ever to play a significant part in Irish politics after his release or escape from Van Diemen's Land. It was refugees in Paris and New York, men such as James Stephens, John O'Mahony and Michael Doheny, who were to form the core of the physical force movement of the future. The very fact of their flight, in the midst of hordes of hunger-stricken refugees, facilitated the identification, in a confused but most effective way, of the rising of 1848 with the contemporaneous potato famine and mass emigration to North America. As early as 1849, even a moderate like Gavan Duffy was accusing Great Britain of genocide and explaining the attempted rebellion of the previous year in terms of an irrepressible uprising against the state's inhumanity. This may have been wildly simplistic; but (much against Gavan Duffy's own intentions no doubt) it succeeded in reawakening and freshly feeding the insurrectionary 'tradition' of 1798, and in reglorifying violent methods.

O'Connellism had dominated Irish nationalism for more than a quarter of a century. Now at last its opposite was beginning to show itself above ground again, this time first and foremost across the Atlantic Ocean. Fenianism was about to take shape.

5

Mid-Victorian Ireland: 1850–70

The Great Famine

What were the causes and consequences of the Great Famine which has been looming over our pages? In the harvests of the early 1840s a new fungoid disease made its appearance among the potato crops in North America and then in Europe. This was *Phytophthora infestans,* popularly known as 'blight', and it was at the time and for many years thereafter an incurable plant disease. It reached Ireland in September 1845, and rapidly destroyed much of the crops still in the ground over roughly half the total area of the country. In 1846 and again in 1848 the failure was virtually complete in the majority of regions. In 1847 and 1849–52, there were partial failures, as well as much reduced sowing, particularly in 1847. About one million persons (out of a population of some 8 500 000) died of starvation and deficiency diseases or accompanying epidemics during these years. Well over one and three quarter millions (possibly some 1 900 000) emigrated, if we extend the 'famine' period to 1855, as we probably should, to allow for the facts that a season's emigration partly depended upon the preceding season's harvest; it took at least two further seasons before even the immediate chain-migration effects of Irish departures made themselves fully felt. This was the famine emigration. Beneath its stark figures of departures, and of deaths and disease in the attempts, lie reefs upon reefs of human sorrow, never more piercingly expressed than in the simple anonymous Gaelic verses:

> My grief on the sea,
> How the waves of it roll!
> For they heave between me
> And the love of my soul!
>
> Abandoned, forsaken,
> To grief and to care,
> Will the sea ever waken
> Relief from despair?

With one important exception, the famine had little direct effect upon Australia. Irish emigration to Australia was still governed by the Australian demand for people rather than the (now virtually limitless) Irish supply. In fact, it declined instead of increasing in numbers during the famine years. But it did include one unusual and most significant component, the importation of approximately 4000 orphan girls, from Irish workhouses, into New South Wales, Victoria and South Australia. These girls, nearly all teenagers and the indirect victims of the famine, were recruited (out of many more thousands of applicants) to correct the sexual imbalance in the colonies, and more particularly to mitigate the shortage of domestic servants. Their hoped-for ultimate destiny was marriage, and no doubt many tens of thousands of today's Australians are to be counted among their descendants. They were a notable infusion to the youthful female population of the time,

The principal effect of the famine on Irish Australia was symbolic. For many Irish emigrants of the next generation, it symbolised a vast national failure and disaster, for which the British government, as the self-appointed administrator of the Irish economy, was held principally to blame. In the case of Irish-Australians, however, this became simply an item, albeit the major item, in the catalogue of grievances

Emigration to Australia was much more effectively regulated and protected than that to North America. The government embarkation depot at Birkenhead was run by the Colonial Land and Emigration Commission.

against the oppressive power. It had little or none of the traumatic effect on them that it exercised throughout the nineteenth century on Irish-American activists. For such Irish-Americans the Great Famine was synonymous with a desperate mass migration under cruel conditions, a headlong flight of economic refugees, victims of countless sufferings and miseries permitted if not actually contrived by the British government. There was no Australian counterpart. Still, even for the Irish-Australians, the catastrophe of 1845–52 became and remained part of a resentful folk-memory.

The famine years had profound long-term as well as immediate effects on Irish society itself. If it did not inaugurate, it greatly speeded up the movement away from the pattern of subdividing holdings, marrying early and depending on the potato as the principal or sole source of food. From 1850 on, this pattern was gradually replaced by its opposite over all but the poorest regions of the country.

In the new pattern, the number of very small holdings was drastically reduced, as was the number of agricultural labourers, while the cottier class was virtually eliminated. Instead, both landlord and surviving tenant were tacitly agreed on one aim at least—to keep intact and if possible enlarge farm size. This was accompanied by a willingness to postpone marriage where necessary—and it was generally necessary—to avoid the break-up or a multiple tenancy of the holding. Further, the larger farm and higher rent, together with the rapid growth in the British market for meat and dairy products, implied a movement towards a less subsistence and more cash-oriented form of husbandry, in which cereals and the potato gave way, to a considerable extent, to a mixed or essentially stock-rearing type of farming.

The new social and economic pattern had begun to show itself in various areas before the famine, but it did not touch the most impoverished western, south-western and north-western coastal parts for another generation. But, taking Ireland as a whole, the famine transformed agrarian habits in a remarkably short period. The small farm, to be held together at all costs as long as the tenant lived, worked by family labour and passed on intact to the eldest or most favoured son, became typical in the Irish countryside. Even with the post-1850 increase in average farm size, however, the number of people a holding could sustain was very small. This meant that, normally, only one member of the family (the one destined to inherit) would stay permanently on the piece of land. Occasionally, unmarried brothers or sisters also remained, accepting, for whatever reason, the near-penniless condition of dependence this entailed. As they were growing up, children of course had to help with farm work, especially at harvesting and (to a lesser degree) sowing times. But it was increasingly the rule that most of them should leave home in their middle or late teens: there was little room for extra adults on small tenancies. This 'surplus' was generally destined to migrate to the towns and cities, Great Britain or overseas. Few became paid agricultural labourers, the demand for whose services fell dramatically during and after the Great Famine.

Correspondingly, subdivision no longer provided a means of staying in one's native locality. It was now anathema to tenants as well as landlords. Moreover, as rural Ireland became remarkable for late rather than for early marriages, with more and more males awaiting succession to the farm before 'settling down', the pressure for female emigration mounted, and with it the unusual migratory pattern of young single women often constituting the vanguard. Many country girls had little to look forward to at home, with the pool of potential husbands shrinking, and a growing resistance on the part of fathers to alienate any part of the family inheritance for dowries. All this ensured that the outflow unleashed by the Great Famine would continue in very considerable force down to 1914, and that well over half those reared on small farms grew up in the knowledge that sooner of later they would probably have to migrate. By a strange irony, this very emigration enabled many poor holdings in the 10–20 acre (4–8 ha) range to survive 'uneconomically', through the remittances sent from abroad by the departed children.

The other side of the coin was a gradual but steady increase in farm income, and relative agrarian prosperity, from the early 1850s to the late 1870s, because of rising demand for Irish livestock, meat and dairy products in the British market. The cash infusion reinforced the new tendencies towards the consolidation and enlargement of holdings, and their maintenance intact against all comers and every odds. This was all the more so because rents increased more slowly than tenant income. It also meant that when, at last, bad harvests combined with lower agricultural prices to produce a severe agrarian depression, the tenants fiercely resisted the implicit threat to their long and painfully attained higher standard of living.

The fall-out

Although the social and economic fallout of the famine still affected the early 1850s, the two decades 1850–70 are commonly spoken of as a distinctive phase, a 'mid-Victorian' era. The usage 'mid-Victorian' has some point for Ireland, as well as Great Britain itself, at least in the sense that Irish developments matched British more closely in these twenty years than at any other time in the nineteenth century. This is of particular interest for Australian history because of the high proportion of Irish emigrants to Australia who were born or brought up between the Great Famine and the Parnellite epochs.

Modernisation is of course a constant process, but its speed, range and ramifications in Ireland were especially notable between 1850 and 1870. Even in physical appearance the country changed remarkably. The majority of minute and very small holdings outside the western and south-western coastal regions were swallowed up into larger units and bigger fields, leaving a multitude of ruined hovels as mute testimony to a once more densely populated land. Most of the countryside had a much barer look by 1870—at least so far as humans went: they were roughly one-third less in number whereas cattle and other farm animals were roughly one-third more. Irish farming was responding to the cross-channel demand that drove up the prices of cattle, pigs, meat, poultry, eggs and butter by 30–50 per cent, while leaving grain prices more or less at their former levels. More cash in the economy had significant local effects. Towns, especially the small market towns of the interior, grew considerably in size, although the coastal cities, apart from the partly industrialised Belfast and Derry, scarcely changed at all: even Dublin's population increased but slightly before 1870.

A major factor in the increase of Ireland's exports of livestock and foodstuffs to Great Britain, and the consequent swing to a more pastoral Irish economy, was the revolution in transport. The basic railway network had been laid down in Britain before 1850. The Irish equivalent was built between that date and 1870. In 1850 Ireland possessed some 400 miles (644 km) of railway, almost all of it recently constructed, and consisting largely of short radii issuing outwards from Dublin and Belfast. By 1870 this had been extended to 2000 miles (3220 km) of track, and all the main arteries of internal trade were linked. Moreover, at one end of the scale, the roads leading to the major railway stations were being steadily improved, while, at the other, quick, safe and reliable steam-driven vessels completed their conquest of cross-channel communications. Although passenger traffic increased significantly with the advance of rail and steam, the increase in goods traffic was far greater. The trade in live and perishable commodities gained most of all from the transformation.

Commerce moved in both directions. British manufactured and extracted products began to spread much more widely, from the leading Irish port, Dublin, to the provincial towns along the railway systems, and thence gradually into the countryside. Retailing grew fast; local trades and hand-icrafts declined still further. Less palpably but effectively, metropolitan culture and social practices followed the same route as British manufactures. Viewed in one light, this can be seen as an especially rapid phase in 'modernisation'. Looked on in another, 1850–70 may seem an especially rapid phase of 'Anglicisation'. This second categorisation is to some extent misleading. It is true that Ireland was being fitted more tightly into a worldwide economic and political system centred in Great Britain, with London at its very heart. The equivalent was also true of the Australian colonies between 1850 and 1870. In their case, too, the process of being knitted into the imperial fabric was greatly speeded by the remarkable advances in sea and telegraphic communications, and with them a more immediate and direct exposure to metropolitan modes and mores. Colonial self-government did nothing to hinder such a development. If anything, it removed, in the short run, sources of friction with the metropolis which might have been inimical to the spread of central influences of fashion and social usage.

In Ireland the lack of self-government barred the way to any form of Anglophilia, no matter how far Anglicisation of the style of living might have extended. In part (the essentially O'Connellite part), this revulsion was rooted in the denial of Irish people of the powers and rights exercised by their British (and especially their English) equivalents, and in the wish to possess and control a British form or system of government of their own. In part (the essentially Young Ireland part) it derived from the opposite strain in Irish nationalism, which revolted against cultural assimilation to Great Britain and sought to preserve and nurture every distinctively Gaelic or traditional feature of Irish society. To take an extreme example, the *Celt*, a weekly produced in the 1850s by the Celtic Union, was dedicated to combating British cultural supremacy which was destroying 'our national and characteristic identity'. As yet, this nativism had not hardened into a definite shape, let alone become organised to a significant degree. But its main lineaments could be discerned already by even a moderately prophetic eye.

The principal resistant to Anglicisation during 1850–70 was, however, the religion of the majority. These years were marked by a double drive in Irish Catholicism. On the one hand, it was being Romanised, in the sense of coming under more and more central bureaucratic control, ultimately directed by the Holy See. On the other—a somewhat paradoxical accompaniment—it was also asserting itself increasingly as a national church, and indeed claiming to be the principal expression of Irish nationality. Under both heads, organised Catholicism adopted a generally anti-English stance, in the sense of equating English with Protestant, agnostic or other influences hostile to its own mission. The Church had already tended in this direction in the years immediately preceding the Great Famine; but the trend was much more marked thereafter.

Two events at the turn of the mid-century drove it forward. First, a national Synod held at Thurles in 1850 laid down a system of ecclesiastical discipline, and diocesan and parochial order, that was soon to extend over the entire country, and produce an extraordinary degree of religious uniformity and 'efficiency'. Second, Paul Cullen, formerly head of the Irish College at Rome, was appointed to what was virtually the leadership of the Irish Church, first as Archbishop of Armagh (1849) and soon afterwards as Arch-bishop of Dublin (1852). Cullen was *au fait* with the Curia and the entire range of papal policy over the previous twenty years, and he continued to enjoy the friendship of many in high places in Rome. All this inclined him to use his considerable powers and abilities to fit Ireland more closely into 'the Roman mould'. On the other hand, his sense of Irish nationality was strong. He was no conven-tional nationalist. He identified Irishness with Catholicity, and saw Protestant Britain as the enemy of both. Thus, an important side-effect of the decrees of Thurles and the elevation of Cullen was greatly to strengthen the forces opposed to the further advance of English influence in Ireland, especially in anything that might touch even faintly on faith or morals.

Nor was this a matter of Church officialdom alone. The Catholic laity in general was also changing. Proportionately, the strong farmer and retail trading elements in the community were growing steadily. Latter-day critics may see such a development as leading to a cult of respectability and rigid social restraints. However that may be, it also produced (as well as derived support from) a more strictly observant and triumphalist religion. The 'devotional revolution', long before discernible in the cities, towns and areas of urban influence, spread widely both in the number of pious practices, sodalities, processions and retreats being undertaken and in their extension into those country regions not 'reformed' in this fashion before the famine. In one sense, the growth of a respectable and deeply observant laity, with its concurrent social disciplines and subordinations, was quintessentially a 'mid-Victorian' phenomenon. But in this case it formed a most substantial barrier to the inroads of English influence—at any rate, to those forms of influence (and they were numerous) that denigrated Catholicism or Irishism, or both.

The land question

During 1848 one advanced Young Irelander, James Fintan Lalor, had proclaimed the new doctrine of the tactical priority of economic issues. The land question, he argued, would serve as an engine to draw forward the train of national independence. In the course of the next year, Gavan Duffy, as editor of the *Nation*, changed the main direction of that journal from criticism of the political regime to criticism of the agrarian system. A more concerted attempt was made during and after 1850 to switch the focus of Irish political agitation from repeal of the Act of Union (which had in any event lost its driving force with O'Connell's decline and death) to repeal of the legislation and modification of the common law that favoured landlords. The program of the Tenant League founded in that year was popularly summarised as the '3Fs': *freedom* to sell interests in tenancies, *fair* levels of rent, and *fixity* (that is, security) of tenure. Retrospectively, these seem modest aims. Yet they outraged contemporary British opinion. Specifically, they were definitely opposed to two orthodoxies of the day: first, the absolute nature of the rights of property; and second, the argument that dealings in land were on a par with all other sorts of dealings, that they were as simply contractual as any other commercial transaction—from pawnbroking to selling pounds of sugar. Again, the League failed to throw up either effective leadership or a concerted plan of action. Worst of all perhaps, it was invaded by sectarian conflict between its Ulster Presbyterian and its southern Catholic factions.

Although it failed as a political movement, the Irish Tenant League did succeed in redefining the Irish question as well as laying down a new ambit claim on behalf of the nation's smallholders. Land was to be at or near the forefront of Irish agitation from now on. The League was also to have a profound effect—by a process of transference—on Australian, and particularly Victorian, history. Duffy, who was a major protagonist in the League, arrived in Melbourne in 1852, and several of its other leading members also emigrated about the same time to Victoria, where they helped to organise and sustain a fateful League-type movement of land reform. It should also be noted that Peter Lalor of Eureka fame was brother to the agrarian radical, James Fintan, and that their father, Patrick Lalor, had been the chief mover in the most important form of Irish land agitation in the 1830s, tenant resistance to the compulsory payment of Church of Ireland tithes.

Although the League had ceased to operate as a national organisation by the mid-1850s, some branches remained intact down to and throughout the 1860s. There was always a feeling abroad that a general farmers' movement was lurking offstage, ready to take to the boards should any undue pressure be placed upon that class. Partly in consequence, evictions were few and far between, even though it was within this period that the notorious Derryveagh 'clearance' from Co. Donegal, which led to a minor wave of popularly-assisted emigration to Australia, took place. The great majority of Irish landlords, faced with actual or potential tenant organisation, did not press for a proportionate share of the increased agricultural profits of these years. Their restraint was the real token of the tenants' power. A secondary manifestation of the improvement in their relative position was the importance of the farming vote in Irish county elections from 1852 to 1868. The farming 'middle class' had gained considerably from an Irish franchise reform in 1850, and was sufficiently organised to have a significant influence in a number of rural electorates.

This did not result in any really concerted pressure for Tenant Right (the new movement for land reform) in the House of Commons between 1850 and 1870. After O'Connell's death in 1847, Irish nationalist politics had no single direction, but were rather a medley of ill-connected aims. Nevertheless, the tenant cause was always represented, to some extent, by the handful of Irish MPs who had either given pledges to their farming constituents or were otherwise involved in the land question. This persistent if not especially vigorous agitation bore fruit in an unexpected quarter in 1865 when the noted economist, J.E. Cairnes, burst forth as an advocate of Irish peasant proprietorship, expressing in his theory of landlord–tenant co-ownership the fundamental presupposition underlying Tenant Right. Once leading English radicals such as John Stuart Mill and Henry Fawcett took up Cairnes's idea, the Irish land issue was well on the way to the forefront of British politics at last. It would have to await, however, the reordering of the parliamentary scene after Gladstone's victory in the general election of 1868 before this could be translated into attempted remedial legislation.

Parliamentary entanglement

Between 1850 and 1870 party discipline was weak in the House of Commons, with no government enjoying a secure majority for long. Even Palmerston's administration of 1859–65 was subject to many alarms and excursions. The Irish MPs—except for the small groups who were right-wing Conservatives—both reflected and contributed to the relative instability. The disintegration and eventual disappearance of O'Connell's Repeal party left a vacuum filled by various overlapping and often rival interests. Tenant Right and the reform of the system of land tenure remained, as we have seen, a persistent strain. Catholic issues also weaved in and out of mid-Victorian politics. Such issues took many forms. Initially, an Irish faction was formed to oppose the Ecclesiastical Titles Bill of 1851, itself the product of a British Protestant counterattack against supposed popish designs on the faith of the British people. The Irish Catholic Church mobilised itself, of course, in 1851 to counter the anti-Catholic legislation, even if the matter was largely one of mere names and symbols. The Church was outraged that, in the season of its apparently victorious advance, a measure formalising its inferiority and purporting to crush its pretensions should be proposed. At the other end of the little epoch Archbishop Cullen and his confreres (and the considerable body of Irish MPs whom they influenced) fought strongly in the campaign that led to the ultimate disestablishment of the Church of Ireland in 1869. There is a certain neatness in all this. From having its drive towards parity checked by the furore over ecclesiastical titles at the outset of the phase, 1850–70, the Catholic Church in Ireland ended it as legally the complete civil equal of its traditional and once-omnipotent adversary. In between, various 'Catholic' political issues came before the House of Commons. Often

101

these were concerned with such cross-cultural matters as the control or content of education or the chaplaincies of public institutions. More important than the specific issues was the tone or colour of Irish political engagement itself, well discerned by an acute and experienced observer, W. J. O'Neill Daunt, who wrote in mid-1859, 'Whatever public spirit exists in Ireland just now is religious rather than political'.[12]

A third factor at work among the Irish MPs was the desire to form an independent opposition, that is, to act in concert but without any regard to—let alone collusion or cooperation with—either of the major British political groupings. This was in part a reaction to O'Connell's generally predominating policy of seeking a 'Whig alliance' whenever the Liberals were in reach of or in possession of power, and in part an expression of disenchantment with Russell's 1846–52 administration. The Independent Irish Party, as a coherent body, was dealt a crippling blow as early as 1852–53 when some of its members accepted offices offered to them by the British government. But as a political objective, and in vestigial form, it survived down to the 1860s and constituted throughout the period yet another cross-issue subdividing the Irish nationalist representation in the House of Commons.

Such a welter of major aims and the absence of any truly controlling leader or leaders led to the operation of personal influence at the polls. Both landlords and priests were able to direct voters in various ways to a degree unprecedented since O'Connell's rise. It greatly depended on local conditions whether particular interests pitted themselves against one another, or were monolithic in form, or took the field at all. Nevertheless, these were golden years for landlord and priestly power, especially among the county electorates. They were also golden years for pork-barrel politics in the boroughs. Candidates often stood for election and were returned on some quite local issue, or some supposed economic benefit to the constituency that needed state expenditure or other governmental action to be set in motion.

In many ways Irish parliamentary politics during 1850–70 resembled those of the Australian colonial assemblies down to the 1890s. The major differences were two: Irish factions were at once looser and more lasting than their Australian counterparts; and unlike Australians in their little groups, Irish members could never hope to be part of a government *en bloc*, even if individuals might occasionally be recruited to give a government some momentary tactical advantage. In theory, the principle of independent opposition, to which so many paid lip service, should have barred the way to mere association with, let alone membership of, any British government. In practice the Liberal party exercised a fatal magnetism for almost all Irish nationalist MPs during these years. In the end, the Liberals could count on their support in the vast majority of cases, although this is not to say that the survival of the catchword of 'independent opposition' was of no significance. Ideals can be cynically disregarded, and yet live on to fight another day.

As to the Irish Conservatives, the mid-Victorian interlude proved prosperous politically. They even won a majority of the Irish seats in the general election of 1859. Of more significance in the long run was their capture of more and more of the Protestant urban vote in Ulster, which had hitherto been mainly Liberal. Already, the cities of Belfast and Derry were being divided geographically according to religion; Orangeism was making heavy inroads into the Protestant working class; and populist Toryism was emerging. Several of the leading features of Northern Ireland politics in the late twentieth century had begun to appear clearly by 1870.

The Fenians

The feebleness of the 'constitutional method' in the 1850s and 1860s opened the door for its historic rival. Revolutionism had gradually revived in Ireland over the years 1844–48 because of three convergent developments: the glorification of past deeds of valour; growing shame at the subservience and appeasement of OConnell's current politics; and the inevitable entry of the gun on such a scene. The next stage in the process was to occur overseas. Military failure in 1848 and the general depression that accompanied the famine scattered many of the proto-revolutionaries of the late 1840s both east and west, in particular to France and the United States. In each place, ideas were coloured and developed by local circumstances. The eventual junction of the two separate streams had to wait practically a decade, until 1858. When it came, 'Fenianism' (to use an imprecise but indispensable term largely synonymous with the IRB or Irish Republican Brotherhood) was the result.

Dominant in the French stream was James Stephens, who had sought refuge in Paris in 1848 after his escape from Ireland. Stephens was a classical nineteenth-century revolutionary conspirator unshakeable in his faith in ultimate success, visionary, tyrannical, vain, suspicious and single-minded. He was not the man to acknowledge indebtedness to others. But in two respects his later ideology matched contemporary Parisian modes so closely that it seems reasonable to infer some measure of derivation. First, the Paris of the Second Republic was the international capital of insurrectionists, many of them the debris of the failed European revolutions of 1848–49. Here conspiracists of the old Continental type regrouped, and absorbed the lessons of defeat. In this milieu, Stephens could well have found his particular version of the secret oath-bound society dedicated to the overthrow of established government. It was a highly schematic form of organisation, minimising the dangers of the informer in its ranks, and maximising central direction.

Stephens' second possible Parisian debt may have been to neo-Jacobinism, as expounded by Blanqui in 1848 and later years. Blanqui, an extreme republican in the

104

revolutionary tradition, eschewed social and economic objectives, and concentrated on the actual seizure of power and the overthrow of 'illegitimate' government. The Blanquists saw themselves as acting for 'the People'. No matter if they were in a popular minority: this merely meant the postponement of elections until the 'mission of democratic enlightenment' had changed sufficient minds. Stephens left no political testament, but his own conduct and the stamp he impressed on the later Irish revolutionary movement were redolent of this creed and program.

The other stream of Fenianism, the American, was certainly ambiguous in its early stages. It originated in the New York Emmet Monument Committee of late 1853, the very name of which was meant to imply a link with the United Irishmen and the doctrine of 'England's difficulty, Ireland's opportunity'. With the outbreak of the Crimean War, Nicholas I's Russia had become the (somewhat strange) surrogate for Revolutionary France. In fact, the Russian 'alliance' never materialised. However, the arrival of a new factor in Anglo-Irish conflict had been signalled. This was the formation of an Irish-American 'community', considerable numbers of whom were bitterly Anglophobic. To such people, the United States appeared, on the one hand a secure base in which to plan revolutionary action, and on the other an international power that might be induced to use its influence to reduce or remove British oppression in Ireland.

The American strain of Irish revolutionism in the 1850s was inward as well as outward looking. It was concerned with mustering Anglophobic sentiment in the United States as well as American arms and money; it was also eager for violent action in Ireland and much inclined to images of forces setting sail to land in and liberate the homeland. All this meant an extraordinary degree of 'open' activity for a supposedly clandestine organisation. John O'Leary was amazed, when he reached New York in 1859 as the covert agent of the IRB, to find himself 'serenaded' in public by a brass band of the celebrated '69th New York'; called on to address the crowd of 'conspirators' in the street from the window of his hotel; and finally having his 'mission' reported in the columns of one of the Irish–American papers. It was, as O'Leary said, 'a queer sort of proceeding to give a public, or semi-public, reception to a secret envoy'[13]; but it was inherent in the nature of the Irish-American movement. Such expressive activity was of course also calculated to advance Irish immigrants socially in the United States.

To a marked degree, the IRB, formally established on St Patrick's Day 1858, represented an amalgam of the French and American varieties. Perhaps its most striking feature was its absorption with the revolutionary act to the exclusion of all consideration of the consequences. The nature of Irish society, of the Irish economy, and of religion in Ireland under the new order, were not only ignored, but were also forbidden questions (because potentially divisive or distracting). Even the avowed existence of an 'Irish Republic' may have implied nothing about the ultimate form of government. O'Leary contemplated even dual monarchy, with Victoria as Queen of Ireland as well as England, with equanimity. 'It is not, nor has it ever been with me, any question of forms of government, but simply of freedom from foreign control'. In one sense, this was the key to Fenianism. Its universal, overriding objective, what all Fenians had as their common aim was simply, the eradication of British influence in Ireland. As O'Leary concluded, 'English rule, directly or indirectly, proximately or remotely, [is] at the bottom of the whole trouble . . . and to shake, if not shatter, that rule, was then, and is still, the great aim, or, if you will, dream of my life'.[14]

The core of the Fenian methodology was the resort to armed force, and the steps preparatory to insurrection. In part, such steps were conspiratorial after the Carbonari model; and these were to reach their apotheosis in the prelude to the Easter Rising of 1916 when the innermost circle of the IRB systematically deceived even its own president—to say nothing of its rank and file. But revolutionary preparation also drew upon the American strain, in particular, for the provision of a sea in which insurrectionary fish might not only swim but also be spawned. The Fenians had to hit on means of tapping and channelling the wild waters of indeterminate Anglophobic sentiment in their fellow countrymen if they were to recruit members and popular sympathy. Hence their equal emphasis on propaganda, parade, support groups and shows of strength.

Although the Irish Fenian membership probably never reached as many as 50 000 in number, the organisation did attract a fair proportion of the marginalised young men, especially in the towns—shop assistants, clerks, artisans and labourers. Typically, they possessed some education but neither property nor prospects; and Fenianism provided them with both a means of self-expression and a road to self-esteem as well as a sincere patriotic goal.

Another remarkable feature of the movement was the emergence of a women's auxiliary corps, the Fenian Sisterhood. The corps may have been inspired by experience of the American Civil War—'girls forget[ting] all vanity to make lint and bandages which may serve for the shattered limbs of their betrothed husbands',[15] as George Eliot put it—although it is also true that women had participated indirectly in O'Connell's repeal campaigns. Even if the Sisterhood had little practical importance, the precedent was certainly significant. The Ladies Land League of 1880–81 was for a time a crucial element in the Parnellite movement, until Parnell himself saw it as a challenge to his own control, and brusquely wound it up. In late nineteenth century Ireland national politics opened the door to feminism. The remnants of the Ladies Land League drifted in that direction. Conversely, early Irish feminism was sucked into extremist politics in the 1900s.

Fenianism could never have been formidable militarily unless perhaps—and this was never proposed—it had turned into a guerrilla force. Its arms were few, and mostly antiquated. Yet the mere prospect of an Irish revolution was enough to send a chill of fear through British governments as well as Dublin Castle. Crushing an insurrection might not prove very difficult; but its aftermath and its social and sentimental legacies were a different matter. What hopes then of an enduring Irish peace?

At first the majority of Irish voters and Irish journals, and almost the entire body of Irish Catholic bishops and priests, were strongly opposed to Fenianism. This was partly a matter of traditional allegiance. Both the old O'Connellites and, to some extent, the one-time Young Irelanders regarded the Fenians as ungrateful and narrow-minded upstarts. More important, they saw them as dangerous to the existing social order and established political processes, to say nothing of the lives of ordinary Irish people, should an insurrection and the subsequent repression plunge the country into bloodshed. The memory of 1798 could cut both ways. The institutional Catholic Church had additional reasons for its relentless opposition. Fenianism ignored its absolute con-demnation of conspiratorial societies; and the proposed insurrection fell well short of the theological criteria for 'a just war'. Again, the wayward conduct and internecine quarrels of the Fenian leadership and factions (for which Stephens himself must take much blame) disenchanted many potential supporters, while the repeated postpone-ments of the insurrection blunted the edge of militancy. When the Fenians took to the field at last in February and March 1867, they lacked not only numbers but also clear objectives and authoritative direction. They were easily crushed and almost as easily rounded up.

Fenianism in defeat and humiliation was, however, quite another matter from Fenianism arrogant and bombastic. In the eyes of the nationalist population of 1867, the belated, ill-organised and ill-coordinated risings aroused widespread sympathy for the young men who had failed utterly in the military sense. Such an upsurge of feeling was all the easier because there had been little actual violence or bloodshed.

Pity for the brave deluded rebels, instinctive tribal identification with any armed challenge to Great Britain (after it had actually occurred), and resentment at the counter-measures adopted by the victorious authorities combined to produce a change in Irish mass sentiment. The majority might still condemn the Fenians with their heads, but not any longer with their whole hearts. Because contentious issues arising from the rebellion kept cropping up over the next few years, this ambiguity—or perhaps we should say, dualism—of sentiment remained alive. The popular struggle of the late 1860s for amnesty for the Fenian prisoners well exemplifies the fusion of emotional, humanitarian and political drives that characterised the post-rebellion upsurge of sympathy in favour of the 'victims'.

Another major legacy of Fenianism was the number of members and former members—most of them young or very young in 1867—who led or promoted radical movements in Ireland during 1870–90. Whether or not they abandoned violent and conspiratorial methods, their experience of Fenianism had steeled them for good in an unremitting resistance to British rule in Ireland. By the same token, the resort to arms of 1867 led a few on to political terrorism, in forms new to the Anglo-Irish conflict. Individual assassination and the destruction of life and property by explosives (specifically, dynamite) entered the scene in the 1870s and 1880s. These were, however, rare acts, almost universally repudiated and deplored by contemporary nationalists.

Fenianism began as an international movement, and fittingly enough it attracted much international attention for several years, despite the meagreness of its practical achievement. The United States was of course its 'other home'; it never ceased to have some links with Paris; and it awakened not only amazement and curiosity but also much fear of the unknown and immeasurable in Great Britain. Rumours that the IRB had recruited heavily among regiments with large Irish components were especially alarming. There can be no doubt that these apprehensions

109

added urgency to the cause of Irish reform. Gladstone himself, although in characteristically delphic phraseology, admitted that Fenianism had been the spur to even so critical a measure of change as the disestablishment of the Church of Ireland in 1869.

Almost fortuitously, the Australian colonies were also affected—even if rather in the opposite way—by the phenomenon. First, the well-publicised revolutionary conspiracy in Ireland was used to considerable effect in the internal politics of the colonies. It was most tellingly employed perhaps by Henry Parkes in New South Wales. But the 'Green Scare' was a good card to play at almost all electoral tables throughout the continent. Second, the Rising of 1867 led directly to the resurrection of transportation. Nearly one hundred Fenian prisoners were sent to Western Australia in what was to prove the last chapter of a convict system that had been inaugurated by the settlement at Port Jackson. How ironic, as well as how bizarre, was this! Although it is very doubtful if even a single cell of the IRB ever existed in Australia, the idea—or rather the caricature—of Fenianism and the presence of actual 'heroes' of the insurrection were woven quite intricately into the history and folk-memory of particular colonies.

6

The Age of Parnell: 1870–1900

Parnell and the Land League

The land question had been intermittently significant in Irish politics all through the years 1850–75. For the next decade it was to be all important. Bad harvests in the later 1870s, and particularly the three successive failures of 1877–79, coincided with the cheapening of food imports to Great Britain from abroad, including the Australian colonies. Overseas, cereal and meat production had increased by leaps and bounds; and striking improvements had been made in marketing, sea transport and refrigeration. Ironically, it was Disraeli's Conservative government, then in office, that refused any agricultural protection for the United Kingdom. The urban—increasingly artisan and working class—voter in Britain was strongly in favour of cheap food, and welcomed the consequent fall or stablilisation in the cost of living. But in Ireland the majority of voters were themselves stricken farmers or lived off an economy based on farming. By 1879 the agrarian depression had halved Irish farm income, and although most landlords abated rents because of this collapse, few abated them pro rata and some refused all concessions. The upshot was militant tenant resistance to the rents demanded, and in some cases refusal to pay any rent whatever until a new level of charges was negotiated.

111

Still more abhorrent were the evictions, on which the most diehard or hard-pressed of the landlords attempted to insist. The Irish smallholders were adamant that the advances in their standard of living, so slowly and painfully acquired over the past two decades, should not now slip away. Agrarian violence spread rapidly in the west and south, although, in the main, the tenant movement eschewed the use of force. The crucial step was taken in April 1879 when a Land League was formed (mainly at Fenian and ex-Fenian inspiration) at a meeting at Irishtown, Co. Mayo. Equally significant was the acceptance of the presidency of the League by Charles Stewart Parnell, a young and seemingly radical Nationalist MP who led a small group of intransigent Irish members in the House of Commons. The issues of land reform and political independence had at last been truly fused.

Parnell had entered parliament as a Home Ruler at a by-election for Co. Meath in 1875, at the age of twenty-nine. This was in itself no remarkable achievement although he had beaten Charles Gavan Duffy, one-time Young Irelander and former Premier of Victoria, for the nomination. Parnell was strikingly good looking, a Protestant, a landlord and sufficiently pecunious to pay his own way in the House of Commons. On all counts, he was an appealing candidate. The Home Rule Party, which he joined in the House of Commons, although new as a parliamentary contingent was already dying on its feet. Since O'Connell's death in 1847, Irish political pressures at Westminster had been generally ineffectual. Various attempts had been made to keep the MPs from nationalist constituencies distant from and even opposed to both major British parties. In fact, the Home Rulers represented yet another effort to establish an independent Irish opposition. Each, including the current thrust, failed or was failing, because of the attractions of the British Liberal Party, which could provide Irish members and their clients with places and other minor rewards and occasional legislative concessions. The Liberals had been regularly in

112

THE LAND LEAGUE,

WITH AN INTRODUCTION BY

J. E. REDMOND, M.P.

9415

CHARLES STEWART PARNELL, M.P.

Melbourne:

J. LEWIS, HOT AIR PRINTER, 200 ELIZABETH STREET.

M.DCCC.LXXXIII.

The Redmond brothers' tour of 1883 was backed by Land League propaganda produced in Australia. Parnell was beardless at this time so as to render him less easily recognised in public after he had begun his affair with Katherine O'Shea.

power, with only comparatively short breaks, from 1846 to 1874. Thus, whether nominally independent or not, groupings of Irish nationalist MPs tended sooner or later to become Liberal satellites.

In 1875 the majority of the Home Rule Party was well down the road of conciliation and, ultimately, absorption. But a handful of its members had broken out in the opposite direction, defying parliamentary conventions and obstructing parliamentary business on all possible occasions. The intensely Anglophobic Parnell threw himself into this congenial work, and by dint of a powerful, domineering personality and unremitting diligence soon rose to the command of the small band of intransigents who sought to degrade the institution of which Victorian Britain was most proud, the House of Commons. At the same time, he carefully cultivated the appearance of extremism, and angled for the support, in Ireland and the United States, of the upholders of the physical force tradition by his violence of language and backing for Fenian causes. He was well aware of the dangers of this course. It aroused suspicion and distrust in both the Church and the ranks of moderate nationalism (including almost all the press) at home. It was a calculated gamble in the course of his strike for Irish leadership.

Parnell plunged deeper when he accepted the presidency of the Land League, for the League had kept up its Fenian associations and was committed to withholding rents and fighting evictions, if need be, by boycott and intimidation. But the general election of 1880 fully justified Parnell's daring. He ran 'his' own candidates against the official Home Rulers in several of the constituencies, always with success, and ended up with thirty committed supporters in the House of Commons. There he formed a tightly disciplined party, which, acting as a unit and backed by more or less continuous Irish agitation, changed the face of British politics.

During 1880–82 Parnell and his lieutenants (mostly young men of considerable talent, no social standing and

small means) turned nationalist Ireland into a single concerted movement. The Catholic Church, the better-off as
well as the smaller tenant farmers, the press and the
physical force and ex-physical force men, all coalesced
under his aggressive and ingenious leadership. This control
was nearly absolute, on both the home front of agitation
and the parliamentary front of obstruction and disruption
of the proceedings of the House of Commons. Despite, or
perhaps because of, his own imprisonment in October 1881
(which he may well have engineered himself to avoid
responsibility for the worsening agitation of the winter of
1881–82), he established himself ever more firmly as
national leader; and by a series of brilliant manoeuvres
ended up with a *Land Act* (1881) that in effect conceded
the long-sought '3 Fs'. Supplementary measures in the
following year wiped out huge arrears of rent, and extended
the new concessions to every form of Irish tenancy.

It was a remarkable triumph. In 1870, only eleven years
before, Gladstone's first administration had baulked at yielding any substantial element of the Irish tenant demand. Now
his second administration surrendered the entire original
program almost without demur, and enacted further conciliatory legislation in 1882. In one sense, it was all too late.
The Irish tenants had, in the course of long-continued
agitation and excitement, moved on to a more radical
objective, the transference of the actual ownership of the
land. It was with difficulty that Parnell called the forward
movement to a halt in order to change the point of the
attack to his ultimate constitutional goal, Home Rule. But
in the end, his skill in manoeuvre proved as successful, in
dealing with the Irish rural masses and his own political
machine as it had in dealing with the British political system
in the early 1880s.

Parnell's weapons in the early struggle with Gladstone's
government had been the threat of further disorder, both
in the Irish countryside and at Westminster, and the
unbreakable solidity of his support in each arena. He set

about translating the second, Westminster, into another source of power by holding the balance of votes between the two main British parties. In June 1885 he joined forces with the Tories to bring down Gladstone's government and, as the ensuing general election approached, tried to play off the Liberals and Conservatives against each other. Specifically, he sought a commitment to some measure of Home Rule in return for the Irish votes in Britain under his control, which, it was supposed, could swing up to twenty British seats. Although Parnell failed in his immediate object—even the Liberals refused to promise any move towards Irish constitutional autonomy—his general strategy was vindicated. He threw his support in the British constituencies behind the Tory party in the hope of denying the Liberals an overall majority, and achieved exactly the desired result. The Liberals won most seats, but neither major party could govern without the backing of Parnell's MPs, now eighty-five in number and subject to an iron discipline. Before 1885 was out, Gladstone, restored as Prime Minister, committed himself to the introduction of an Irish Home Rule bill in the coming parliamentary session.

It is difficult for late twentieth century people to realise the magnitude of Parnell's achievement. Only two years before it was scarcely conceivable that three British MPs, let alone 300 British MPs, would ever countenance Irish legislative independence. The very notion ran counter to basic contemporary beliefs in imperial strategy and security, the safety of Protestant kith and kin, and the upholding of the most elemental rights of property, which the Land League was supposed to be endangering. Now a major British party—that moreover had been in office for most of the preceding half-century—had adopted Home Rule as its leading policy. The 'victory' was not to be measured in terms of immediate success (for this was dubious) but in those of apparent long-term certainty.

There was a heavy price to be paid for Gladstone's capitulation. The Liberal Party split, and a considerable number of members went into opposition, never to return to the fold. Conversely, the Conservatives committed themselves the other way; they now called themselves Unionists and gained considerably from it among the English electorate. With the House of Lords as their willing instrument, and Queen Victoria herself by now a Tory partisan, their blocking powers were formidable indeed. Parnell too had a stiff price to pay. The Home Rule Bill proposed by Gladstone was a very modest measure, affording little more autonomy for the proposed Irish Parliament than a state government enjoys with regard to Canberra today. Parnell had moreover to accept it unreservedly and as 'a final settlement' before the Gladstonian Liberals would throw themselves wholeheartedly into its support.

Again, he proved to have made the right choice. British observers had expected much opposition from both Irish and American extremists; but there was practically none. Parnell argued that, as leader of the Irish people, he had a mandate to negotiate on their behalf; and such was the personal command and control that he had established over the preceding five years, that he succeeded almost without exertion. Immediately, the new move failed. A sufficient number of Liberal MPs had rebelled to ensure the defeat of the Bill in the House of Commons. Worse, Home Rule was the chief issue in the ensuing general election of 1886, and in Britain the anti-Home Rule forces swept the polls: English opinion was particularly hostile to Gladstone's procedure. But the long-term prospects were good and steadily improved.

The Liberal alliance

From 1886 on, the Liberal and Parnellite parties were firm allies. This went far beyond the earlier compact between the two, the so-called ' Kilmainham Treaty' of 1882 whereby Parnell and his colleagues were released from prison in return for the diminution of agitation. It went far beyond even O'Connell's bargain with the Whigs during 1835–39. From 1886 on, every Irish measure in Parliament received full Liberal support; and, for the first time, the whole system of British government in Ireland was criticised, and often opposed, by one of the great British parties. Such a running fire rendered the current attempt at wholesale coercion largely ineffectual. In fact, the new Conservative government suffered the worst of both worlds. As self-proclaimed strong men, they had to keep up the facade in Ireland. In fact they were generally on the defensive because of the heavy parliamentary pressure to which they were subjected. For Parnell, this was the ideal situation. There was enough repression to sustain Irish militancy, but not nearly enough either to destroy Irish organisation or revive Irish militarism. Irish militancy without Irish militarism had always been Parnell's objective. He had once pointed out that it was a great mistake to suppose that Ireland could not be effectively coerced, but added that this would never happen while Britain was divided by its two-party system.

At any rate, having ruled out the genuineness of the Irish cry for legislative independence as a mere catchword peddled to them by their charlatan politicians, the Tories were impelled to provide an alternative mode of governing Ireland—the mode later to be known as 'killing Home Rule by kindness', although the phrase itself had been coined long before. The theory was that the Nationalists could be outbid on purely political and constitutional issues if one provided sufficiently generous economic and social reform. Hence the paradox that the major legislative concessions of the late nineteenth century (from an Irish Nationalist point of view) came from the Tories rather than the Liberals. Not least was this noticeable on the issue of land itself, where the agitatory pressures produced further rounds of reduction in the levels of rent, further Acts wiping out arrears of rent and, most important of all, the beginnings of effective land purchase schemes and the transference of the land to those who worked it. The Tories were also to attempt the economic and social reinvigoration of the so-called 'congested districts', the most barren and poverty-stricken areas in Ireland. This marked a most significant advance in modern state planning and investment. In Irish Nationalist terms, the years 1886–92 and 1895–1900, Tory years, produced considerable gains, equal perhaps to the total achievements of the first eighty-five years of the Act of Union. Certainly, in the decade of the 1880s, Parnell's decade, more was achieved than in the preceding three-quarters of a century.

Meanwhile Parnell's policy was making headway even on the largest issue of them all, Home Rule. The tide turned against the Tories soon after at the general election of 1886. There followed an unbroken run of Conservative defeats at the string of by-elections of 1887–89. By 1890 it seemed certain that a new election could not be long postponed and highly probable that, when it came, the Liberals would be swept back to power on the Home Rule issue, and the battle then transferred to the House of Lords. A few weeks in the autumn of 1890 destroyed all these prospects.

Since 1881 Parnell had kept Katherine O'Shea, the wife of an Irish Liberal MP, as his mistress, and had children by her. Probably in the hope of financial gain—and possibly with the connivance of, or conspiracy by, the Tory central office in London—O'Shea at last took divorce proceedings at the very end of 1889 and, in the following autumn, succeeded, with Parnell cited as co-respondent. It was an accepted convention of contemporary British politics that any person publicly shown to be an adulterer must leave public life. That such a person should remain as a political leader seemed inconceivable. It was only three years before that Sir Charles Dilke, the likeliest successor to Gladstone and the leadership of the Liberal Party, was ruined politically in circumstances very similar to Parnell's. Parnell, however, treated this convention as he treated other British conventions. He determined to defy it from the outset and, after several lengthy periods of disengagement from affairs, he now suddenly became a whirlwind of activity. By a series of rapid and ruthless manoeuvres he secured a re-endorsement as Chairman from his parliamentary party and browbeat the Irish nationalist press by the same means. Then he checkmated, in effect, the Catholic hierarchy and priesthood. They privately disapproved of the retention of Parnell, as indeed did a majority of the Irish MPs and an even larger majority of Irish editors. But by making no immediate public pronouncement, the Church was practically acquiescing in the decision.

This left only Gladstone and the Liberal Party to be conquered or out-manoeuvred. At first it looked as if Parnell's audacity might triumph here, as well. The majority of both the Liberal leadership and the Liberal rank and file might well have submitted, however distastefully, if the chain reaction had kept going. After all, Gladstone and several members of his Cabinet had known about Parnell's liaison for years and had indeed used Mrs O'Shea as an intermediary. The situation changed decisively, however, when the nonconformist organisations spoke out. Nonconformity was as vital to the British Liberal Party at most stages in the nineteenth century as the trade union movement is to labour parties of the present day. When the nonconformist press and leaders threatened directly not only to desert the Liberals but also to fight them if Parnell was retained as Chairman, Liberal organisations throughout Great Britain, from top to bottom, were in peril. Gladstone yielded to the pressure. In effect, he told the Irish Party that he would be forced to resign unless Parnell was immediately deposed.

The Irish Party was now left with an agonising choice, and Parnell did nothing to ease the choosing. He fought unscrupulously and indefatigably; he would accept no word of compromise; he would not resign. He used all the skill of obstruction, which he had once employed to devastating effect in the House of Commons, in the parliamentary committee room in which this battle raged. Although he was, in the end, dismissed from the Chairmanship by a near 2:1 majority, he continued his struggle with satanic fury. The Irish Catholic Church, the Irish nationalist newspapers— with a few exceptions in each case—and the bulk of the Irish electorate were against him. He lost each by-election in the remaining year of his life—again, by hostile majorities of, on average, nearly 2:1. But he fought unwaveringly until his sudden and tragic death in October 1891. He died believing that within four years he would once again become what he had earlier been called: the uncrowned king of Ireland.

The next major Irish constitutional politician, Arthur Griffith, was a lifelong Parnellite, yet, interestingly, the two tactics against which he always set his face were the cult of personality and the Westminster method (that is, the concentration of Irish agitation in the House of Commons); and these were the essence of Parnellism. As far as Parnell himself was concerned, the writing was on the wall as early as 1886 when he forced his party to hand over the Irish Nationalist seat of Galway City to the hated O'Shea—presumably because O'Shea was blackmailing him over his liaison. From 1887 onwards, Parnell had become increasingly reckless and arrogant. He began to ignore Parliament for months on end. He disappeared mysteriously. His lieutenants and followers heard nothing from him, even in times of crisis. He lived under false names. He was contemptuous of all possible Irish opposition. All this rested on the well-grounded assumption of his own indispensability as the engineer and the guarantor of the Liberal commitment to Home Rule of 1886; and, in the fullest sense, the engineer was hoist with his own petard when the Liberals secured his removal from the Irish leadership. So, like a Greek tragedy, the nation and the leader moved to a doom together, a doom apparently implicit in the dangerous relationship that had developed between the two.

The aftermath was disastrous for conventional Irish nationalism. Ten years were to pass before the new divisions, conflicts and personal hatreds, compounding the old divisions that had been released again, began to die down: they never died away completely. Home Rule was a lost cause for almost two decades. Meanwhile much of the old ineffectuality returned. The reason for all this was simple. By 1890 the whole Irish strategy had been concentrated for almost five years on one thing, the Liberal alliance. There was no alternative strategy available or likely to be developed for a considerable time. Thus, it was not at all surprising that the majority of the Irish Nationalist MPs should have concluded that to defy the Liberal Party would be to destroy all prospect of Home Rule in the nineteenth century.

The 'alliance', however, depended heavily on the personal standing and authority of the respective leaders, Parnell and Gladstone. The Irish Party was accustomed to Parnell's virtually uncontrolled direction; and no other Liberal could command anything like the respect and obedience that Gladstone had. After the 1890 struggle for the Chair, Parnell not only ceased to provide leadership for more than a fragment of the Party, but also effectively prevented any other from assuming his old position. Worse still was his almost wanton defiance of his own lieutenants, followers and nation, and his reckless, if not deliberate, creation of embittering antagonisms within all these. The second blow fell when in 1894 Gladstone resigned from Parliament after the defeat of his second, revised Home Rule Bill in the upper House. There would never be another crusader for even limited Irish independence within the Liberal ranks.

Parnellism and Australia

Parnell's rise marked the beginning of the period of most intense interaction between Australian and Irish politics. The initial field of Irish nationalist agitation, Tenant Right and rent reduction, had a profound appeal for Irish immigrants

Australians contributed generously to relief funds during the
threatened Irish famine of 1879–80.

to Australia and their immediate families. The preceding
three decades had seen a heavy Irish influx—proportionately the greatest of all in Australian history—and it was
predominantly an influx drawn from the small farming and
agricultural labouring classes. These immigrants had instinctive sympathy with the plight of their counterparts (very
often their own near relations) 'at home' as the agrarian
crisis developed from 1877 onwards. When, after 1881,

123

legislative independence began to replace land reforms as the leading Parnellite objective, it was again a theme with which they could identify with whole hearts. Home Rule could be, and almost invariably was, presented as the sort of self-government that the colonies had already achieved: Ireland was merely seeking what the people of New South Wales, Victoria and the rest currently enjoyed. According to this argument, a domestic Irish parliament was no more inimical to British allegiance and interests than the Legislative Council and Assembly in Macquarie Street, or their equivalents in any other Australian capital.

Down to the 1890s colonial politics worked, not by parties in the modern sense, but by interest or issue groups which themselves often changed in composition, coalescing or dividing continually. Among these, an Irish Catholic grouping was comparatively recurrent, and occasionally of major significance, especially in Victoria and New South Wales. It was generally on the radical side on the issues of land, property and popular government; but it was also, of course, a protagonist of denominational education which was chiefly a conservative cause. 'Irishness' had been a political liability in Australia in that it was generally regarded as anti-imperial and anti-British in tendency. It was also commonly associated with ignorance, superstition and all the other dark forces that made up the tribal stereotype in the minds of the Australian Protestant majority.

Initially, the Home Rule movement deepened this hostility, and accelerated the tendency of the more 'respectable' Irish Catholics to distance themselves from what was presented, in the colonial press, as subversion, violence and sedition. But the 'mission' in 1883 of two able young Nationalists, John and William Redmond, to gather Australian funds and support for Home Rule, proved a turning point. At first widely reviled, refused meeting halls and assailed by leading colonial politicians, they gradually turned the tide. By the conclusion of their long visit to South Australia, Victoria, New South Wales and Queensland, they had set up branches of the Irish National League in many places, collected considerable sums of money for the home organisation, drawn in most of the Irish Catholic middle class to the support of Home Rule, and even produced an abatement of the anti-Irish prejudice among Australians at large.

With the announcement of Gladstone's 'conversion' to Home Rule at the end of 1885, the favourable trends accelerated. For Australian liberals, no less than British, Gladstone was the great political hero of his generation; this was particularly the case with the nonconformists. Hence a sudden but profound change in the standing of, and support for, the Irish-Australian groupings in all the colonies. The years 1886–91 constituted their halcyon days. It gave them an equality of place in the community, an integration into colonial politics, and a respect for their objectives—as wholly in step with those of liberal and radical Australians and enlightened imperialists—such as they had never before enjoyed, and never would again enjoy. During these years, the visiting Irish MPs who followed the trail blazed by the Redmonds were feted, and rewarded with extraordinarily large amounts for the Home Rule cause: overall, in fact, Irish–Australia produced far more money per capita of the population than Irish–America, let alone than the Irish in Great Britain.

All this did not end abruptly or completely in 1891 when Parnell's party split, to the accompaniment of savage recrimination. But the divisions in Irish constitutional nationalism were bewildering and depressing for Australians; and the cooling of British Liberal ardour for Home Rule after 1893, and Gladstone's final resignation in 1894, dissipated most of the exterior support that had been built up in the 1880s. Moreover, the rise of the Labor Party in Australia in the 1890s diverted the Irish-Catholic groupings, to a considerable extent, to domestic issues. The zenith of eager engagement and interest in Nationalist politics in Ireland and Westminster had come and gone.

In Australia, Parnell, however adulated, had been a shadowy figure, never seen or likely to be seen. At home his personal magnetism had always counted; and it continued to reach out from the grave for a decade or more after his death. The bitter struggle between Parnellites and anti-Parnellites left its traces even after the main body of Nationalist MPs was formally reunited in 1900. Indeed these surviving antagonisms explain much of the Party's relative feebleness and continued confusion of purpose after the re-amalgamation. Not only was the party itself debilitated but so too was the whole constitutional mode of politics. When Gladstone's second Home Rule Bill of 1893 was overwhelmingly rejected by the House of Lords, the Liberal Party practically shelved the Irish cause. To many it then began to seem that the life and death struggle to depose Parnell had been all for nothing. However, the great majority continued to march along the familiar roads as if under the old direction.

'Irish Irelanders'

Throughout the 1890s the shell of Parnellism still covered the Irish political scene. Although the party itself broke into two, and for a time even into three, public discourse in Ireland remained much the same. A Home Rule Act was still the goal, Westminster was still the main arena, and the use of massed votes in the nationalist constituencies to demonstrate the Irish popular will was still the designated weapon in the struggle. But beneath and along the edges of the shell new forces stirred.

One significant 'internal' change was the temporary return of the Catholic Church to the foreground of constitutional politics. It was forced to take the lead in the organisation of anti-Parnellism in many areas. Often it did so eagerly, but it was not true that the priests had been merely awaiting their opportunity to destroy Parnell and defame the radicals. Like most of nationalist Ireland, they

126

had opposed him only when it seemed clear that his continued leadership would frustrate the avowed national objective. Nevertheless, 'the church-in-politics' was well and truly back for a time on the Irish scene. Clericalism and anti-clericalism were perhaps more evident, or at least more openly in contest, than ever before in Irish politics—an additional source of communal division, as well as the inspiration of some of James Joyce's most plangent passages.

Meanwhile other forces, of little immediate but profound long-term importance, had been born in the heat or aftermath of Parnell's power. Among these were several concerned with the 'Irishing' of Ireland. The Gaelic League, the Literary Revival and the Gaelic Athletic Association, for example, were all launched between 1886 and 1893, and all sprang from discontent at Ireland's drift toward British cultural and social forms. Parnell and Parnellism had offered no resistance to such a tendency. The orthodox Irish Nationalist of the 1880s and 1890s was scarcely aware that a 'problem' of Anglicisation existed. As Douglas Hyde, the Gaelic League's founder, observed in 1892,

> . . . the Irish race at present is in a most anomalous position, imitating England and yet apparently hating it. It has lost all that they [the old patriots] had—language, traditions, music, genius and ideas. . . we find ourselves despoiled of the bricks of nationality. [16]

Certainly, in the outward forms of life and expression, the distinctively Irish element was in further decline in the last decades in the nineteenth century, and under increasing pressure from British modes and habits.

Hyde intended the Gaelic League to be apolitical, concerned solely with the nurturing and expansion of the Irish language. He failed to avoid politics, partly because his movement was deliberately infiltrated by extremists, and partly because such a movement inevitably manufactured separatists. Some members looked on it as a leisure interest, or joined to discover more about their 'roots'; but for others it became a sort of 'school for sedition', knitting sections of the middle and lower middle classes into a quasi-political association. The effects were profoundly important. Instead of binding Irishmen of all types and opinions together (as Hyde originally had hoped), it drove the wedge between north and south, between Unionist and Nationalist, deeper than ever. It gave new point and precision to Irish self-identity, externalising and symbolising what had hitherto been an undeveloped aspiration in many cases. In the long run, it helped to undermine the Irish Nationalist Party, which bore to its dying day the impress of a pre-Gaelic generation.

The Literary Movement was similarly conceived as apolitical at the beginning. In fact, Yeats positively denounced Irish nationalism insofar as it prostituted art in the name of politics, and spread shoddy literary and cultural standards. There was also in Yeats's mind—and perhaps to a lesser extent in Hyde's—a distinct antipathy to modern urban and industrial civilisation; and the Movement's marked early emphasis on pre-Christian sagas and mythology may have owed something to the desire to counter the assumption that there was a necessary connection between Catholicism and nationality. As a further complication, various participants in the Movement followed various European literary fashions of the day. But despite all these cross-currents and extraneous considerations, it again proved impossible to avoid separatist politics—indeed some of the Abbey Theatre's repertoire expounded them straightforwardly in dramatic form—while to preach nativism and traditional or supposed peasant values was also to help cultivate the type of highly wrought romantic imagination that was to flower with such extraordinary effect in the Rising of 1916.

The third Gaelicising or Celticising force, the Gaelic Athletic Association, differed strikingly in its origin from the other two. It was a mass movement, neither intellectual nor artistic; and it was positively grounded in militant separatism from the start. The GAA sought to insulate native from

British sport, eventually by a system of exclusion and boycott. It was an application of the technique of the land war to a branch of ordinary life with the ulterior purpose of creating and maintaining a different national identity. Thus the Association was at once what the League and the Literary Revival ultimately became—a mechanism that gave new substance, and day-to-day reality, to the concept of a distinct Irish nationality. Once more, this had an ominous implication for Home Rule. A Gaelic Ireland, which played different games, devoted itself to different pastimes and fostered a different popular culture, could only deepen the gulf between the north-east, which clung to the British patterns, and the rest.

Moreover, the Gaelic Athletic Association was immediately and outstandingly successful. It quickly formed a network that, at least outside the towns, touched in some degree a very considerable proportion of the population. The formalisation of traditional games and pastimes was a most opportune development. All over the English-speaking world organised sport was advancing with amazing rapidity in the late nineteenth century. The GAA capitalised on this general trend; and, especially in rural Ireland, it captured the majority of the new generation of players and supporters. Based on parish and county, the Association fitted well into the organisational grid that had served Irish nationalist politics, and to some extent even the Catholic Church, throughout the nineteenth century. It was another dimension of ordinary life that yet reinforced the established local and national patterns.

At the outset, the GAA was presented—as were the Gaelic League and the Literary Movement—as protective and preservative in purpose. Each was meant to nurse the dying embers of one form or other of the traditional culture back to life, with the hope that they would later glow once more and perhaps ultimately spread across the land. Each also implied, and was in fact mainly driven by, opposition to Anglicisation and the rapidly increasing social uniformity of the United Kingdom. Always hostile to rival sports (and for that matter competing dance and music), the GAA formally 'banned' Rugby and Association football, cricket and hockey to its members within twenty years of its inauguration. They were stigmatised as 'Garrison' games, an arm of British cultural imperialism. The same spirit affected new movements which apparently lay beyond nationalistic considerations. Even early Irish feminism, for instance, reflected the same Anglophobia. *Inghinidhe na h-Éireann* (Daughters of Ireland) founded by Maud Gonne in 1900 was similarly dedicated to the eradication of 'low' English literature and theatre, English songs and popular English influence of every kind. It sought, with intermingled fervour, complete cultural as well as political independence.

There were also some Irish-Irelanders (the half-derisive term in common use for cultural separatists of every variety) who did not aim at total political separation from Great Britain. For instance, D. P. Moran, who owned and edited the influential weekly, *The Leader*, scorned those who deluded themselves that Britain could ever be forced to relinquish her grip on her dependency. 'All we can do', he wrote, 'and it should be enough for us, is to remain Irish, and to work out our own destiny in the very many fields in which we are free to do so'.[17] Moran, like Griffith, was no admirer of the Literary Movement, or indeed of any form of leadership provided by dissident members of the old Protestant Ascendancy. For him, as for Griffith and, we might add, the rising Catholic middle class as a whole, the day of that Ascendancy was over. Parnell should be the last of his line. The Catholic majority no longer needed the direction of their hereditary 'superiors'; and it was now quick, often over-quick, to detect Protestant condescension and Protestant exploitation of peasant naiveté.

Despite these divisions, the cultural separatists of every kind had much in common. In particular, they enjoyed a common enemy, in the process of Anglicisation, and a common objective, in striving to hold back and, if possible, reverse its onslaught. The reaction to the Boer War showed this clearly. All these groups and movements (though not necessarily all their individual members) were strongly pro-Boer. Support for the Afrikaaner republics seemed a heaven-sent opportunity for expounding the rights of small nations and denouncing the wrongs of British imperialism and British capital accumulation. Nor were these feelings and attitudes confined to the extremists. Most ordinary Irish nationalists were only too pleased to indulge their under-lying Anglophobia in such an apparently righteous and costless fashion. Public bodies dominated by the Nationalist Party freely passed votes congratulating the Boer leaders on their early successes in the campaign.

In this respect, the contrast with the Australian colonies is marked. In Australia the Boer War was generally regarded as an imperial cause with imperial strategic implications, and therefore one that called for a full loyal contribution. On the other hand, the formation of Australian contingents, and their fate and fortune in South Africa, tended to deepen and vivify the sense of separate Australian identity—all the more so as the federation of the colonies into a single state was at last accomplished during the course of the war itself. This Australian move towards a more independent stance had its contemporary Irish counterpart. The original reasons for the change in sentiment were very different in each case—deriving in Australia from an imperial response and in Ireland from the innate repugnance of the majority towards the British Empire. In Ireland, the Boer War restored some of the old acerbity to traditional Irish nationalism but benefited the Irish-Irelanders most. Their organisations, though still (the GAA apart) minute in numbers, all grew in size as the war continued. More important, they coloured the general outlook to a significantly increased degree. In consequence, Irish politics, temporarily at least, took on a more radical complexion than they had shown for several years.

Sinn Fein

The Boer War had also a side-effect of much subsequent significance in Irish history. In 1900, Arthur Griffith set up *Cumann na nGaedheal*, later to become Sinn Fein, as well as the Irish Transvaal Society. Griffith had returned recently from South Africa, where he had been a fervent advocate of the Boer cause: hence his organisation of a support society after his return to Dublin. The future Sinn Fein was an Irish-Ireland body with a vengeance. In addition to the usual calls to foster the native language, arts, music, games and mindset, and equally to combat 'anything tending towards the anglicisation of Ireland', Griffith especially emphasised the need for economic independence. Irish goods were to be bought, Irish natural resources to be systematically tapped, and Irish crafts and industries to be developed. He also had in view that Sinn Fein should serve as a sort of umbrella association to which cultural separatists of all—perhaps we should say of all *congenial*—kinds could attach themselves in time.

Sinn Fein was probably the most significant of the new movements. Touching almost all the rest, it was yet the only one of its kind. Alone it offered a complete political strategy and addressed itself directly to the great constitutional issues. Although his personal inclinations were separatist, Griffith advocated a dual monarchy of Great Britain and Ireland, partly because of the successful precedent of the Austro-Hungarian Empire (or so he said), but also because the retention of British monarchical forms seemed indispensable if the north were ever to be conciliated, and if Irish independence were not to destroy Irish unity. He was remarkable among Irish nationalists for his clear perception, and frank admission, that Ulster was the major problem, and equally so in devising emollient proposals such as a subordinate but distinct Ulster assembly and the weighting of representation in Ulster's favour. Griffith's nationalism was as fierce as any Fenian's, and he had belonged earlier to the IRB. But he was ready to face unpalatable facts. He was also opposed to violent revolution as both hopeless of victory and wasteful of human life.

The three positive elements in Sinn Fein, as worked out by Griffith, had appeared before in Irish history, but only in vague and inferential form. The first was the withdrawal of all Irish members from the House of Commons and their re-assemblage in Ireland as a native parliament. Both O'Connell and Parnell had threatened some such move but each had shrunk from it in the end. The second was the assumption of executive powers by the new Irish body, so far as might be practicable from case to case. To the extent to which this succeeded, British administration in Ireland would become ineffective and die of inactivity. Ultimately, the new 'state' might secure international recognition. Finally, Griffith looked to popular mass action, passive resistance and voluntary involvement in the native system to sanction the new departures and to stultify British power. Sinn Fein, therefore, anticipated, if it did not actually inspire, several characteristic devices of anti-colonialism as it developed in the second and third quarters of the twentieth century. It was also destined to supply some of the prerequisites of success in the Irish situation of 1917–21. All this was for the future. In 1900 Griffith's was only one of a chorus of voices crying new wares to replace the old and tired.

Despite the advances made during the course of the Boer War, most of these voices were still unheeded by the great majority, and often derided as the calls of cranks. The fortunes of the parliamentary party (or parties), of land purchase and local government reform, of orthodox Home Rule—accompanied by the constant, if now faint, contrapuntal theme of conspiratorial republicanism—still engrossed the main Irish public. Nevertheless, the new voices were gradually working a hidden but profound change. They were providing an alternative concept of nationality and independence. When, through the chances of politics and war, their moment came, they could provide

133

the fresh formulae and standpoints that the unaccustomed situation needed. They might have proved mere interesting historical curiosities but, as things turned out, they were to be the ripening forces of the future. It was not to be expected, however, that Irish Australians, as a whole, should have been *au fait* with, let alone sympathetic to, the cultural separatists. If concerned at all about such questions, they had their own indigenous culture to be fostered, a culture in which the important Irish constituent was essentially O'Connellite and Parnellite, rather than Sinn Fein, in character.

7

New Ireland: 1900–22

The Party without Parnell

While great political systems have an extraordinary capacity to absorb new developments, they may also collapse with an equally extraordinary rapidity. To look no further back than the present century, the fall of such 'ageless' empires as the Russian or the Austro-Hungarian, or of apparently iron totalitarian regimes such as the Third Reich or the Soviet Union, shows how swift and sure the final end may be. Even the United Kingdom provides a minor, muted counterpart in the unexpected and catastrophic decline of the party that had normally governed in the period 1830–1914, the Liberals. In Ireland, the Nationalist Party followed more or less the Liberal path, although its reign was shorter and its demise still more precipitate.

The national system constructed by Parnell and his subordinates in the early 1880s oversaw and managed much of the public and some even of the private life of Catholic Ireland—that is, of those regions where Catholics constituted a clear and unassailable majority. By 1890, the 'Catholic' area formed in effect a one-party state, or more precisely a one-party opposition to the state; and the Parnellite/anti-Parnellite division of 1891 did not alter its condition fundamentally. The new factions never put down deep roots. The

135

pressure from below to reunite the Party was much too strong for this. Ironically, Parnell's own stress on the necessity for absolute Irish solidarity had too powerful a popular effect for a lasting break to seem endurable. The healing, in 1900, of the split arising from Parnell's defiance of the majority of the Party was generally regarded as a long overdue rather than fortuitous restoration of the status quo. Reunification appeared all the more urgent then because (perhaps in an effort to kill Home Rule by kindness), the Conservatives had democratised Irish local government in 1898, thereby opening up new tracts of patronage, propaganda and influence to the Nationalists in most parts of the country.

The very junction of the main factions in 1900 was testimony to the underlying strength of the old national system. It had been indirectly challenged by the United Irish League founded by William O'Brien (a moderate anti-Parnellite) two years before. In the League, O'Brien attempted to rekindle the fighting spirit in Irish politics by a major agitation for the extension of land purchase, and a vigorous resistance to the spread of grazing, in the west. The League was spectacularly successful, but O'Brien, true to his political upbringing in the early 1880s, used this success to increase the pressure on both Parnellites and anti-Parnellites to come to terms, rather than in attempting to create a new national movement of his own. In effect, the United Irish League became an arm of the restored Irish Party.

The Party also proved flexible enough to accommodate another significant independent nationalist organisation, the Ancient Order of Hibernians. The Order had originated as a Catholic defence association in the wake of renewed sectarian violence in the north of Ireland in the 1880s. Gradually it developed into a right wing form of constitutional nationalism which practically identified Irishness with the Catholic religion and operated a patronage machine of its own; it also began to spread beyond the boundaries of Ulster. Yet like the UIL it never threatened to become a rival to the Party which eventually used it as a quasi-satellite organisation. The Order never bid for, or even contemplated bidding for, parliamentary representation in its own right.

Between 1900 and 1914 the Irish Party received only one exogenous challenge to its formal political hegemony. In 1908 Sinn Fein ran a candidate against the official Nationalist nominee in a north Leitrim by-election, and lost heavily. It never attempted another trial of strength until after the Easter Rising of 1916. I use the term 'exogenous' because Timothy Healy and William O'Brien, who won a few Nationalist seats for their factions before 1914, had been among Parnell's earliest lieutenants and remained true to the cause of Home Rule, as traditionally defined. Their gains at the expense of the Party were essentially 'schismatic', not 'heretical'. The spell of the 1880s still held its potency. The national system continued its near-blanket coverage of the constituencies, and of all forms of local government.

Nevertheless, the Irish Party had been grievously weakened by the events of 1890-91. In the first place, it had been constructed about Parnell himself, and not only could there be no replacement for the Uncrowned King but also his ghost and epic image served as a constant reminder of the inadequacy of his successors. Besides, Parnell had played a double role; he was national as well as Party leader; and national leadership was, almost by definition, out of reach for any of the quarrelling warlords of the Party he left behind him. It was certainly out of the reach of John Redmond, the faithful Parnellite who succeeded to Parnell's old position as Chairman in 1900. In neither public persona nor political genius could he come within hailing distance of the Master.

It was an ageing Party that Redmond commanded, and especially an ageing inner cabinet. Every member of the Party who was prominent in 1912 had been prominent already in 1882. The once-Young Turks had lost their militancy with the years; and Redmond's plight in this regard was all the worse because John Dillon, the former leader of the majority anti-Parnellite faction, regarded—and indeed imposed—himself as Redmond's equal rather than his second-in-command. All this meant a political hardening of the arteries. The most magnanimous and creative of Parnell's original lieutenants, William O'Brien, who tried to devise new strategies to deal with the obvious difficulties facing Home Rule in regard to the Irish Unionists, was cold-shouldered and effectively driven from the Party in the end.

Again, the Party had owed much of its early success to the shock of its initial impact on the parliamentary system. By 1900, the system and the Party had adjusted to one another, which process robbed the latter of the last vestiges of its quasi-revolutionary character. The emasculation of the Irish Party had occupational even more than social causes. The routine of committee and similar bread-and-butter work in the House of Commons wore away its distinctiveness year by year. Besides, once resistance to Home Rule had been fixed and hardened in the Conservative program, Parnell's original conception of a wholly independent Party was vitiated. The Irish Party might still swear that it was totally indifferent to British politics and ready to make and unmake governments solely in accordance with Irish interests. But by 1900 it was only too apparent that for Home Rulers to make a Conservative government or unmake a Liberal one was simply to cut their own throats.

Even a Liberal domination in the House of Commons— now that Gladstone was gone—by no means guaranteed that Irish Home Rule would stand high on the agenda. This was shown clearly when the Liberals returned to power with an overwhelming majority in 1906. The utmost offered by the Cabinet was the Irish Council Bill of 1907, so meagre a concession that the Irish Party had to reject it out of hand. It took the most extreme pressure from Redmond on the eve of the first General Election of 1910 to exact a pledge from Asquith that the Liberals would recommit themselves to Home Rule should they be returned to power.

*Redmond visited Kalgoorlie during his fund and support raising
tour of Australia in 1904. Rosebery, a leading Liberal, had
proposed the shelving of the Home Rule issue.*

Finally, not only was Redmond's leadership of a much
lower order than Parnell's but also it was peculiarly ill-suited
to his followers. He never suggested, as Parnell had always
done by the very nature of his personality, that responsible
government of Ireland might be but the first instalment of
larger gains. In fact, Redmond had a strong sense of Empire
(both he and his brother Willie had married Australian girls,
Dalton cousins). He would probably have opposed anything
beyond responsible government within the Empire as
strongly as he opposed the Act of Union. 'Let us have
national freedom and imperial strength and unity,' he
declared, from the heart. Contemporaneously, Griffith
described the Irish Party's activities thus: '103 Irishmen in
the House of Commons face 517 foreigners . . . [on a]
battleground . . . filled with Ireland's enemies'. As the
common reaction to the Boer War had shown, most Irishmen sympathised instinctively with Griffith's view, and
recoiled instinctively from Redmond's allegiance to Empire.

There was, therefore, a hidden dichotomy between the ultimate aspirations of the party leader and the led. Nor, indeed, would many members of the led identify themselves, as he did, with any political structure that was British. These divergences, though occasionally manifest, were not really significant before 1910. From then on, when Home Rule had at last become politically practicable, they began to count increasingly. Redmond was inhibited by his own beliefs from enlisting Irish militancy as an ally. This both weakened him in negotiations with the British Cabinet and gradually disenchanted Irish opinion with both his methods and his ends.

Home Rule at last?

The two general elections of 1910 were a bitter disappointment to the Liberals. They lost heavily to the Conservatives, each party ending the year with 272 seats. But Redmond's highest hopes were fulfilled. The Irish Party, with eighty-four seats, held 'the balance of power'. Theoretically, this was the ideal Parnellite situation, even if it was inconceivable that the Party would use its king-making powers to place the Conservatives in office. Moreover, not merely the Liberals but also a new fourth group, the forty-two Labour members, were wholly pledged to Home Rule. This represented an effective 126 majority for the measure in the House of Commons. Finally, the *Parliament Act* of 1911 ensured that the House of Lords could only delay, and could no longer destroy, Home Rule and that the latest date to which they could hold it up was the summer of 1914.

In several respects the 1912 Home Rule Bill fell short of Irish desires; but in the first flush of victory, it was the principle that seemed to matter. Here at last was the prize; it had cost forty years of toil, and many tears. Redmond's reception at the subsequent National Convention in Dublin was tumultuous; for the hour he belonged to the line of Irish heroes. Certainly, the Bill was an advance upon the

Religious distribution in Ireland, 1911

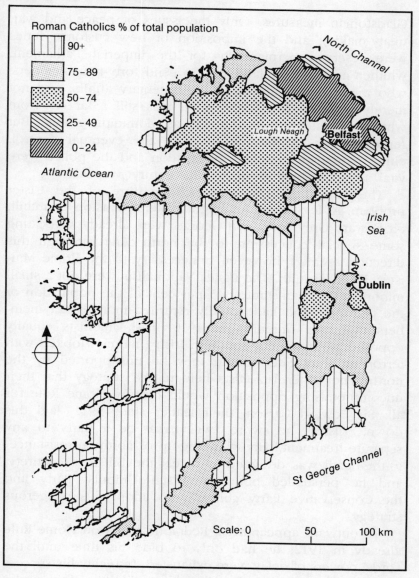

Roman Catholics % of total population

- 90+
- 75 – 89
- 50 – 74
- 25 – 49
- 0 – 24

Atlantic Ocean

North Channel

Lough Neagh

Belfast

Irish Sea

Dublin

St George Channel

Scale: 0   50   100 km

Gladstonian measures. Only the issues of peace and war, treaty-making and the imposition of new customs duties were reserved permanently for the imperial Parliament, whither moreover Ireland was to send forty-two members, who might participate in all parliamentary affairs, and not merely those of Irish concern. It was still a far cry from what was later to be known as dominion status. But representation at Westminster, and the eventual control, either partial or complete, of taxation and the police were vital advances on the nineteenth-century proposals.

The Liberal cabinet was not unaware of the Ulster problem. At least three leading ministers, Winston Churchill, Sir Edward Grey and Lloyd George, were already advocating some special concession to the north. Any move in this direction seemed, however, unnecessary to the Prime Minister, H. H. Asquith. The Ulster Nationalists were not a small minority. They constituted 45 per cent of the population of the province, and had actually returned more Ulster members than the Unionists in 1910. The Unionists equally opposed partition. The southern Irish Unionists looked with terror on their fate, should they be unsupported by the north. The Ulster Unionists held to the strategy that their uncompromising opposition would destroy Home Rule for all. Sir Edward Carson, their leader since 1911, laid this down. 'Ulster', he swore, 'will *never* be a party to any separate treatment.' His whipping-up of northern resistance-to-the-death was designed to defeat the Bill in its entirety; and he persuaded both the Ulster Unionist Party and the Conservative Party generally to adopt this dangerous strategy.

To outward appearances, Redmond had won Home Rule already in 1912; he had only to bide his time until the Lords' powers of delay were exhausted. In reality his success depended on whether the Liberals would stand firm under menaces. As late as September 1913, Home Rule still seemed safe. Asquith rejected an eleventh-hour Conservative offer to attempt a compromise. He argued that even if Carson was not bluffing, Home Rule would bring 'organised disorder but not civil war in Ulster'; whereas if Home Rule were abandoned, the rest of Ireland would be 'simply ungovernable'. Perhaps Home Rule really was secure so long as the balance of fears, in Asquith's mind, was tilted in its favour. But before 1913 was out, not only had Carson formed an Ulster Volunteer Force (UVF) to resist by force the imposition of Home Rule but also a counter force, the Irish Volunteers, was launched in Dublin, in defiance of Redmond's wishes.

This signalled a serious weakening of Redmond's authority. It also meant that, with the sudden likelihood of war in Ireland between private armies, the Liberal Cabinet listened more sympathetically to proposals of compromise. In the transformed situation, an old scheme of Lloyd George's, that Ulster be exempted from the operation of the *Home Rule Act* for a number of years, gained in attraction. Under oblique Liberal pressure Redmond had to surrender some of his paper gains. If he resisted absolutely, he ran the double danger that Asquith would use this as a justification for postponement, and that the growing militancy at home would generate much more radical demands than the 1912 Bill could satisfy. Reluctantly, he agreed that any Ulster county might opt out of Home Rule for a period of six years.

Immediately, Redmond's concession led to a Liberal resolve to force an amended Bill through. Former waverers such as Lloyd George and Churchill now turned on the leading Conservatives for preaching treason and sedition. The Unionist response, however, was to raise the stakes. The Ulster Volunteers began to prepare for real war, most dramatically by running in 35 000 rifles and 3 000 000 rounds of ammunition at Larne on 24 April 1914, while magistrates and other forces of public order stood by complacently. Again, Asquith weakened. Not only did he not retaliate in Ulster—and the root cause of all the Liberal troubles was their failure to tackle the problem of the northern

143

Volunteers—he compounded his error by his feeble handling of the Curragh 'mutiny' of regular Army officers. In short, when faced in 1914 with an apparent determination in Ulster to resist Home Rule by force of arms, the Liberal cabinet again gave way.

Redmond was once more the victim. First, as the violence in the north went unchecked, counter-violence in the south mounted. The Irish Volunteers increased rapidly in number, and Redmond was forced to take on the formal leadership of the movement, in a desperate attempt to maintain control. The second consequence for him of the new Liberal retreat was the Buckingham Palace Conference of 21–24 July 1914. Redmond was coerced into the weakness of further negotiations, after he had already bargained away some of his earlier achievement. Of course, the Conference failed. Neither Redmond nor Carson could have carried his followers with him on the only conceivable compromise, a partition of the island—Redmond, for obvious reasons, and Carson, because he could not have secured more than the four most Unionist counties at this juncture. Liberals and Conservatives alike were rescued from the now-terrible Irish embarrassment by the outbreak of the First World War, which, so to speak, enabled the impasse to survive. The Home Rule Bill reached the statute book in September 1914, but it was not to operate until peace returned, and meanwhile provision for its amendment was guaranteed. The original problems of 1912 were handed on intact to the postwar world.

The Easter Rising

Strangely enough, it had been from pro-British rather than nationalist sources that the ancient cause of physical force returned to Ireland. The immediate reason for the revival of militarism was the formation of the Ulster Volunteers and the 'chatter' about armed resistance among English Conservatives. The IRB, which had undergone a major reorganisation after 1900, ostentatiously welcomed Carson's move. They professed to admire his 'realism': certainly they approved his contempt for parliamentary processes and numerical majorities. Moreover, his action provided them with an opening for turning Irish nationalism back again towards more violent courses. The establishment of the Irish Volunteers in November 1913 had been virtually stage-managed by the IRB. Using leading members of the Gaelic League, especially Eoin MacNeill, as 'front men', the Brotherhood intended to control the new body through Sean MacDermott and a very recent and most important convert, Padraic Pearse, who occupied key positions in the first executive.

These early hopes were disappointed. MacNeill and other moderates acted independently and, so far from breaking with the Nationalist Party, invited its cooperation. Redmond seized the chance, as he saw it, of neutralising this danger on the left. He insisted that half the Volunteer executive should be composed of Party nominees. The proviso scarcely enabled him to control the movement, especially when various sections acted autonomously, in (for example) gun-running. But at least it reduced to very small proportions the number of the IRB men on the executive, and still more in the rank and file, which grew to almost 200 000 after Redmond associated the Nationalist Party with the movement.

It was the outbreak of the Great War that saved the day for the extremists. The war was only seven weeks old when Redmond took the fatal step of committing Ireland to support the cause of the Allies unconditionally. His initial policy, the use of Volunteer forces, northern and southern, to defend Ireland's coastlines by themselves, coupled with an Oath of Allegiance to the Crown, had the support of even the extreme nationalists. But in an extraordinary about turn on 20 September 1914, he ordered his Volunteers to 'account for yourselves as men not only in Ireland itself, but wherever the firing line extends, in defence of right, of freedom and religion'. To what extent he was moved by his own underlying imperial loyalty, or War Office pressure, or political calculations about British opinion, is unknown. What is certain is that Irish nationalism was ultimately offended.

Redmond's prestige and the great weight of the party's organisation still generated such momentum that almost nine-tenths of the Volunteers followed the new lead, many to the extent of hieing to the Flanders trenches. But as the casualty lists grew longer, and war weariness and war cynicism developed, Redmond's breach of the historic principles of regarding not British, but Irish sentiment, and regarding not the common causes but the basic enmities of the two countries, brought inevitable retribution. Since no general election was held between 1910 and 1918, the progress of disenchantment with the Nationalist Party cannot be accurately charted. But the speed with which Sinn Fein advanced after the initial hostile reaction to the Easter Rising amply demonstrates how support for Redmond had been eroded by the end of the second year of war.

Shortly before Redmond's declaration of 20 September 1914, a small group dominated by the IRB had met secretly in Dublin and resolved to stage a revolution before the war concluded. They intended to use for this purpose whatever sections of the Volunteers they could induce to join them. Their task was simplified by a split in the Volunteers after 20 September. The hard core who repudiated Redmond's lead (at most, 12 000 or 15 per cent of the whole number) were, almost by definition, militants. Even so, the majority of them might have opposed the Rising had they had foreknowledge of its occurrence. The three leading officers in the organisation, including the commander-in-chief, MacNeill, conceived its function to be strictly defensive: they would take up arms only if an attempt were made to enforce conscription. This meant that the difficulties of the conspirators were extraordinary. Apart from keeping the principal officers of the Volunteer Council in the dark,

Dublin Castle had to be deceived, and the landing of German arms and the outbreak of the rebellion to be coordinated. As a result, the Rising went off at half-cock, with only one-fifth of the expected revolutionaries in the field and no significant provincial (let alone German) assistance for the Dublin rebels.

A week of fighting in Dublin, ten days of almost desultory executions, 3000 'rebels' shipped to Great Britain for internment, and it was all over—apparently. Of course, all parties were shaken out of the strange trance that had descended once the Home Rule Bill was passed (with assurance that it would never come into force unchanged). Asquith had now to revise his strategy of shelving the entire issue till the war ended. Redmond and Dillon, the Nationalist leaders, could no longer dismiss the Republicans as mere paper patriots; they could not but see that parliamentarianism must now bear fruit soon or perish. The Ulster Unionists exclaimed that the Rising had verified their assertion that Irish nationalism must by its very nature turn to treason. None of them saw the Rising as more than a warning signal. Their existing attitudes were revitalised, but they failed to understand the event in its general historical perceptive. For new apostolic witnesses had now joined the old.

> But who can talk of give and take,
> What should be and what not
> While those dead men are loitering there
> To stir the boiling pot?

> You say that we should still the land
> Till Germany's overcome;
> But who is there to argue that
> Now Pearse is deaf and dumb?
> And is their logic to outweigh
> MacDonagh's bony thumb?

> How could you dream they'd listen
> That have an ear alone

For those new comrades they have found,
Lord Edward and Wolfe Tone,
Or meddle with our give and take
That converse bone to bone.

Indeed the significance of the Rising is missed unless the long past is taken into account. The Rising has been justly termed an IRB rebellion; and the IRB tradition derived ultimately from the French Revolution of 1789. The historical accident that doctrinaire Irish nationalism was born in the 1790s had stamped Republicanism and Romanticism on its face for ever. The basic French concept of the Sovereign People, and the Jacobin gloss that it was the party alone that discerned the people's real will, were faithfully repeated in all subsequent Irish revolutionary movements—or rather in *the* Irish revolutionary movement, as men like Pearse, claiming an apostolic succession from Tone and Emmet, would have said. We should also bear in mind the internal logic of the revolutionary ideas. If the movement was the rightful interpreter and determinant of the people's will, and if the Irish Republic was not a distant objective, but a living, though hidden, reality, then it followed that the legitimate government of Ireland was vested in the movement's leadership, and that the British forces in Ireland were an enemy army of occupation holding down a subjected though unconquerable land. The Proclamation of Easter Monday declared that the long usurpation of government by a foreign people had not destroyed, and never could destroy 'the Irish Republic as a sovereign independent state'.[18]

It was at this point that other, neglected modes of exerting Irish pressure became significant. Sinn Fein had differed radically from revolutionary Republicanism. It was non-violent; it did not seek a republic; its immediate plan was, not insurrection, but the withdrawal of all Irish members from Westminster and their reconstitution as an Irish Parliament. Apart from their common contempt for the ineffectuality of the Irish Party and the inadequacy of Home Rule, the extremist movements were mutually exclusive. But they were also mutually dependent. Sinn Fein would have been nothing had not the drama and emotional repercussions of the Rising melted the moulds in which Irish mass opinion had been fixed. On the other hand, mere insurrection was a dead end. What was to follow, beyond fresh sacrifices in other generations? Revolutionary Republicanism desperately needed something like the Sinn Fein methods, and emphases on moral force, civic organisation and the legitimation of radical courses by popular endorsement at the polls, if any further headway were to be made. The junction between the two forces, initiated in the fighting of by-elections after the rebellion, was consummated at the close of 1917 when Eamon de Valera, the sole surviving commandant of the Easter Rising, became president of both movements—thereby creating in effect two arms, the military and the political, of a single national front.

Ironically, the 1916 Rebellion had given Redmond, temporarily, new hope. Asquith, visiting Dublin in May, acquired fresh resolution when he promised that Home Rule would become immediately operative once 'the different parties in Ireland' came to agreement. The negotiations to this end were left to the supreme broker, Lloyd George, who eventually succeeded in forcing Carson and Redmond to accept common terms—but only on the basis of contradictory assurances to the two. When eventually the truth emerged, each declared, with justice, that he had been grossly deceived, but to Redmond's protest against the chicanery, Asquith merely replied, 'The important thing is to keep the negotiating spirit alive'. He knew his man: Redmond—it might be his epitaph—could not stop parleying.

Asquith himself fell from power in December 1916, but his successor, Lloyd George, was no less eager to encourage 'the negotiating spirit'. It was in his interest to do so. Sinn Fein candidates had defeated the Nationalists at three recent by-elections, and this trend must be checked at once. The government, desperately short of men, wished to extend conscription to Ireland; but without some quid pro quo this could not be applied. More serious still, Britain now depended on the USA for her war effort, and American support might be imperilled if there were not at least some show of concession to Irish nationalism. These were the pressures that produced Lloyd George's 'offer' of May 1917 to set up an Irish Convention to hammer out an agreed solution.

The Convention was a strange agglomeration, nearly 100 in membership. All the Irish parties, including Sinn Fein, were invited to send representatives. So too were the main Churches, commercial interests, trade unions and county councils. Lloyd George guaranteed to adopt its report if there were 'substantial agreement'. It was a riskless undertaking. How could so heterogeneous a body devise an agreed procedure, let alone a solution? The Convention represented a mere variation on the tactics employed by the British government since the Buckingham Palace Conference in 1914. These were, essentially, to throw the onus of reaching a compromise upon the Irish antagonists. In the event, Sinn Fein was the main beneficiary. By boycotting the Convention, it gained in the general estimation when, inevitably, no agreement was reached, and the causes of compromise and negotiation were correspondingly discredited. A more material advantage was the release of the Republican prisoners, incarcerated in Wales after the Rising, as an initial gesture of goodwill when the Conference opened. This made possible the thorough reorganisation of both the political and military arms of the extremist movement without serious hindrance from Dublin Castle.

Redmond died on 6 March 1918. In death at least, he had matched Parnell: his tragedy was classically neat. He had spent his last reserves of health in a desperate struggle to keep the Convention in being and to induce the British government to act as a government and throw its great weight upon the side of settlement. Instead, to appease a clamouring in Great Britain, it assumed, on 16 April, the power to enforce conscription upon Ireland. The Cabinet could have hit on no device more certain to destroy all hopes of an Irish agreement—nor one more worthless, for no one ever dared to use these powers. The first result of the *Conscription Act* was the withdrawal of the entire Irish Party, under Dillon's leadership, from the House of Commons. The 'parliamentary method' had at last run its course. The essence of the original Sinn Fein program had been precisely this step, and Dillon's move blurred the traditional distinction between Nationalists and Sinn Feiners.

The next stage further injured the Nationalists. In the broad-based anti-conscription movement launched immediately in Ireland, it was the militants who seized the initiative. It was de Valera who devised the anti-conscription pledge, with its significant reference to the Act as 'a declaration of war upon the Irish nation', and its instruction to the Irish people 'to resist by the most effective means at their disposal'. It was also he who secured the public, unequivocal approval of the Catholic hierarchy. The final touches needed to ensure the elevation of Sinn Fein were supplied by the British government. The organisation was proscribed as a dangerous body; and on the basis of an imaginary German plot nearly one hundred of its leading members were imprisoned. The Irish Party had now received its *coup de grâce:* the last hope of recovery was gone. In the general election at the end of 1918, they won only two seats in open contests against Sinn Fein candidates, a terrible conclusion to almost forty years of mastery—or perhaps we should simply say that the national system had been at last replaced.

Partition

Sinn Fein seized the opportunity provided by the return of seventy-three of its members to Parliament to make certain that there would be no turning back. Those members not in prison or in hiding assembled as Dail Eireann in Dublin on 21 January 1919. There they confirmed the existence of a Republic, asserted that British administration in Ireland was 'foreign' and illegal, and elected a new, 'legitimate' government from their ranks. This was unmistakably revolution. Yet neither side was prepared immediately to resort to arms. The Dail's program of action, so far, involved no more than an attempt to substitute its own civil rule for that of the existing government, and the winning of international recognition for the new state at the Peace Conference of Versailles.

The situation changed decisively in April 1919 when de Valera, who had been elected President and already designated a Cabinet, introduced a motion that, in effect, licensed violent assaults on the police and other Crown forces in Ireland. From now on war was inevitable, and by the end of 1919 the IRA offensive had already reduced the effectiveness of the RIC and weakened the government's control of rural Ireland significantly. Dublin Castle's response—the proclamation of twenty-seven counties and the mass arrests of hundreds of known (and accessible) Sinn Fein sympathisers—was patently insufficient, and Lloyd George was forced to try another tack and attempt to wrest the initiative from the Republicans.

The cause of the Republic had already suffered, almost unnoticed, a grievous setback. The original strategy had centred on securing international recognition and bringing external pressure to bear on Britain to accept the new Irish 'government' as a *fait accompli*. But the Irish bid to be recognised internationally at Versailles failed completely. A second, and even heavier, blow fell early in 1920. Lloyd George at last determined upon a positive Irish policy, which consisted essentially of a major counter-offensive against the Republican guerrillas and a *Government of Ireland Act* creating two Irish parliaments, for the twenty-six and the six counties respectively. This last probably spelt ultimate defeat for traditional Irish nationalism, although its full significance was concealed until the Boundary Commission was wound up in 1925.

In 1913 the Ulster Unionists had prepared a Provisional Government for the north to seize power when the Home Rule Bill reached the Statute Book. Now they were presented with the same self-government that they had originally threatened to declare. It is significant that the British government did not press seriously for a truce in Ireland until the Northern Parliament had been formally established. Thus before the fighting was halfway through, the Republicans had probably lost half their battle. The *Government of Ireland Act* made it almost certain that *both* full independence and suzerainty over the whole island were unattainable: a choice would have to be made. Perhaps this was the underlying truth of the situation since 1885. But not until the 1920 Act was passed, and a Home Rule government installed in the one corner of the island that opposed it, was the Unionist position quite impregnable.

Meanwhile, the other arm of Lloyd George's new policy enjoyed varied fortune. Its failure was not absolute. From the beginning of 1919 until the early summer of 1920, the war had gone very much the rebels' way. Not merely was the RIC demoralised but also an indigenous legal and administrative system had superseded British government over much of nationalist Ireland. The balance of Irish fear, as well as the balance of Irish sympathy, was tilted deeply in favour of the Republicans. Already the British forces, not to add the RIC, had met terror with counter-terror, with burnings, looting and random killing. Nevertheless, the increase in 1920 of the British army in Ireland to 50 000 men, and the recruitment of thousands of special armed police (the notorious Black and Tans and Auxiliaries) in Great Britain, certainly checked the disintegration of British rule.

It is difficult to strike a military balance-sheet for the last year of the war, from the summer of 1920 to the summer of 1921. One can scarcely say that the position of the IRA improved. The new repression was much more brutal and effective than the earlier counter-terror. When the truce came on 11 July 1921, Sinn Fein had fewer than 3000 men 'in the field', and was desperately short of arms and ammunition. Conversely, the British strategy was self-defeating. During much of 1920–21, the government threw the

Better Not Plant Those

Even in popular radical circles in Australia, Sinn Fein was widely condemned during 1919–21 as violent, divisive and sectarian. Australian public opinion in general agreed, often with additional anger at the blow it was striking at the Empire.

154

reins over the horse's head, tacitly abandoning control of its Irish forces: the evident calculation was that the less the actions of the forces of law and order were supervised, the sooner the 'murder-gang' would be destroyed.

In the long run the official outrages alienated rather than satisfied British opinion. The government's use of censorship and propaganda (both techniques immeasurably improved by wartime experience) made it difficult for the Sinn Fein version of what was happening in Ireland to obtain a hearing. But gradually the government's reputation sank, in Great Britain no less than abroad. 'The whole world', as Chesterton wrote, 'thinks that England has gone mad'; and in England itself the practices of repression began to be condemned not merely by the parliamentary opposition (Labour and Asquithian Liberal), but also by independent Tories, newspapers and ecclesiastics. And as so often, Yeats expressed wonderfully the Irish view.

> Public opinion ripening for so long
> We thought it would outlive all future days.
> O what fine thought we had because we thought
> That the worst rogues and rascals had died out . . .
>
> Now days are dragon-ridden, the nightmare
> Rides upon sleep: a drunken soldiery
> Can leave the mother, murdered at her door,
> To crawl in her own blood, and go scot-free . . .

Moreover, after nearly two and a half years of fighting, Great Britain was as far away as ever from complete success. By June 1921 the government had reached the unpalatable conclusion that the pacification of Ireland required the Boer War methods of great 'sweeps' across the countryside, and chains of blockhouses, which might involve an additional 100 000 men at an additional cost of perhaps £100 million per annum. Faced with the choice of throwing far more men and money into the struggle or attempting to negotiate a peace, Lloyd George plumped for negotiation.

Much has been made of the difference in political quality and experience between the British and the Irish delegations who eventually met for peace negotiations in London on 11 October 1921. Certainly, the British principals—Churchill, Chamberlain, Birkenhead and above all Lloyd George—were the master politicians of their day, even if the leading Irish delegates—Griffith and Collins—showed unexpected capacity as negotiators. As important as the abilities of the respective delegates was their standing *vis-a-vis* their governments. Lloyd George was his own master and could pursue a predetermined strategy. In the absence of de Valera, who refused to attend the conference, come what might, the Irish delegation was instructed to refer all significant issues to the Dublin Cabinet for decision. Meanwhile, they did not know exactly to what ends they should work or what minimum was acceptable to their Dublin colleagues.

The negotiations involved four main areas of conflict: fiscal and economic autonomy; executive and military autonomy; constitutional autonomy; and finally—eternally—Ulster. On the first two issues, the Irish delegates gradually won the day. The British concessions—one might almost say capitulation—in these two areas of dispute were the product of long and difficult bargaining. Some were held up by Lloyd George until the final night of the conference, obviously to retain some quid pro quo with which to match the sacrifices that he demanded of the Irish. These last lay in the field of constitutional autonomy. The key problem, as it seemed at the time, was whether and to what extent Ireland should recognise the British Crown. For each party, this was the decisive symbol: vital for the British, if any remnant of imperial sovereignty were to survive; vital for the Irish, because they saw the Crown as the emblem of their servitude.

In the end, it was the Irish who gave way, though not quite in unconditional surrender. Their retreat was Lloyd George's masterpiece as negotiator. On the final night of the conference, 5–6 December, he presented his antagonists with the immediate choice of war or peace. Selected stage props—trains and destroyers on the ready to bear the news, and alternative letters written in either sense—helped to create an illusion of urgency. It was in a feverish atmosphere that the Irish finally accepted British sovereignty. Lloyd George had succeeded in his principal objective. Dominion status was his minimum demand; he could not hope to carry anything less in either his Cabinet or the House of Commons. But his victory was qualified and, in the long run, at great cost. The Irish delegates had sensibly avoided any precise definition of dominion status. Instead, they tied Ireland's powers and rights to those that other dominions—in particular, the most independent, Canada—might enjoy from time to time. Clearly, the dominions' advance in constitutional status was not yet spent, and the Irish were now guaranteed a place upon the escalator. Moreover, they could themselves speed up the disintegration of the imperial ties.

Lloyd George had taken a perilous step in forcing a state, bitterly hostile to Great Britain, to stay within the boundaries of the Empire. Canada and South Africa were politically divided countries, but each contained powerful British sections. The Irish Free State would be practically united in Anglophobia. In an imperial system that depended ultimately upon mutual sympathy and consent, and was correspondingly weak and unspecific in formal organisation, the Irish had considerable scope for destructive operations. Griffith and Collins were ultimately justified in arguing that they had won 'the freedom to win freedom', to whatever limit the separatist impulse might require. They might also have argued—though in fact a total silence was observed upon the matter—that some shadow of imperial allegiance, some obeisance to the British Crown, was indispensable if the north-east were ever to be joined politically with the remainder of the island.

The last major issue at the conference, Ulster, was handled disastrously by the Irish. Past experience suggested

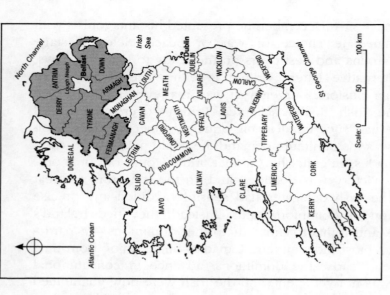

Northern Ireland as constituted by the Government of Ireland Act, 1920

As the map above indicates, roughly one-third of the land area of Northern Ireland, as it was to be constituted by the Government of Ireland Act in 1920, was represented by Nationalist or Sinn Fein MPs at the time that measure

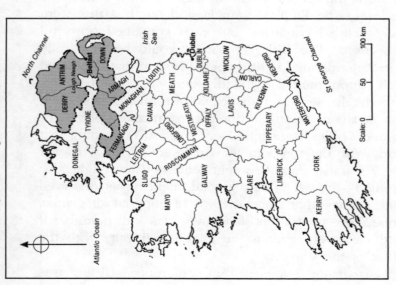

Area with Unionist majorities according to the General Election of 1918

Two urban constituencies which returned Nationalist or Sinn Fein candidates in 1918—Falls, Belfast and Derry (Londonderry) City—are included in the shaded area.

that it would prove the least tractable of all. Yet it was far from the forefront of the discussions. Instead, the Irish delegates concentrated on defence, finance and, above all, constitutional relations. Part of the explanation was Lloyd George's control of the course of proceedings. He had long before prepared his checkmate: with a Northern Ireland parliament in being, he could always disclaim sole, or even prime, responsibility for the fate of the north-eastern counties. His second precaution was obtaining, on 12 November 1921, a secret undertaking from Griffith that he would not refuse to sign a treaty *merely* because of disagreement on Ulster. Having already acquiesced, Griffith was suddenly confronted on 5 December by his own self-denying paper. Once he adhered to his original undertaking, the pressure on his colleagues to concur was great, and in domino fashion they fell one by one.

Lloyd George achieved this result by dangling before the Irish eyes the prospect of eventual Irish unity through a commission to adjust the border between north and south. Naturally the Irish delegates were tempted by the prospect of one-third or more of the northern territory being incorporated in the Free State, with the further assumption that the remaining fragment would prove 'non-viable'. But they neglected to insist on two seemingly obvious precautions: neutral international adjudication and clear instructions to the adjudicators as to the principles on which territory should be transferred. Instead, they accepted a commission composed of one British, one Northern Ireland and one Free State nominee, and a phrase that left the commission free to determine the border on practically any criterion they wished to choose. The blunder was due partly to the inexperience of the Irish delegates, but mostly to the fact that the issue came to the forefront only at the eleventh hour, which in turn derived from de Valera's desire to 'break the negotiations'—if break there had to be—on the Ulster question. As so often happens, the chateau brigadier proved to be the deluded strategist.

8

New states: 1922–45

The Irish Free State and Australia

The Treaty and its acceptance in June 1922 by a clear majority of the electorate in the newly formed Irish Free State marked the end of close Irish-Australian interest in the course of Irish politics. Although that interest had never again attained the level of 1885–91, it had remained moderately high, with occasional intensifications, until final attainment of dominion status for the twenty-six nationalist counties of Ireland. The Irish Party was well supported financially down to 1914, and Redmond was generally accepted in Australia as Ireland's leader well after his authority had begun to crumble at home. Such time-lags were to be expected, all the more so as the Australian commitment to the 1914–18 war was much deeper and more enduring than that of even Redmond and his like. Archbishop Mannix's lead in the Australian anti-conscription campaigns should not be taken to mean that Irish Australians quickly appreciated the significance of the Easter Rising or that they veered about to back the Sinn Fein party straight away. In fact, Patrick Clune, Archbishop of Perth, was probably more representative of Irish Australia, and of Australian Catholics as a whole, than his more celebrated Melbourne counterpart.

Clune, who had been born in Co. Clare, was a moderate Home Ruler who threw his weight behind Redmond and the Nationalist Party both before and throughout the war. In 1914 he became the Catholic Chaplain-General to the Australian forces, of whom he met large numbers in France and England in 1916, to the accompaniment of widespread acclaim for his humanity and understanding. It was not to be expected that he would be an instant convert to the causes of Republic and Revolution (with German aid) in Ireland after the Easter Rising; nor was he. Yet when, in the course of a visit to Europe in 1920, he travelled through the disturbed south-west of Ireland, he was horrified by the atrocities being committed by the British forces, and for a considerable period strove to act as intermediary between Lloyd George's government and the Dail in an effort to bring the fighting and destruction to an end. In Paris, on his way home, he spoke of the IRA as the cream of their country's youth, and on his return to Perth publicly denounced Britain's Irish policy.

In all this, Clune was probably a faithful reflector of the variations in Irish Australians' attitudes as they reacted to the twists and turns of Irish events: these were, of course, brought to them—in the first instance, at least—mainly by the British press. By 1921 sympathy for Sinn Fein, as against the old Irish Party, was very common in their ranks. But the Treaty seemed to almost all Irish Australians (to say nothing of Australians in general) to provide virtually the same independence that they themselves enjoyed. They could not comprehend the reasoning or motivation behind its rejection by de Valera and the Republican minority. Still less could they identify with the precipitation of a civil war in Ireland. For the majority, the Irish political case was closed in 1922. The Crown and the North might be left to posterity to settle. Catholic and nationalist Ireland was free at last—or if not absolutely free, well, near enough was good enough, after all.

Yet the very turn of events that diluted Australian interest in Irish politics rendered the new Irish Free State important to Australia's constitutional development. Between 1922 and 1937 the Free State led the way in reducing Britain's power and status within the Empire. This was one area in which the Irish separatist drive continued to gain ground. Griffith and Collins were vindicated in their argument that the agreement of 1921 set no bounds to the march of the nation. Of course the tide had turned already in their favour. The later stages of the 1914–18 war, and the postwar peace negotiations, had seen a diminution of Great Britain's dominance in the imperial structure. Nevertheless, even if they were rowing with the current, it was the Irish, principally, who manned the oars and drove the vessel forward. Australia did little to assist the process of imperial disintegration—and apparently had little desire to do so—during the 1920s and 1930s. But willy-nilly its relative constitutional independence grew as the Irish hacked away at one after another of the links binding the dominions to the 'mother-country'.

From the first, the new Irish government (headed by William Cosgrave after the deaths of both Griffith and Collins in August 1922) pressed for international acceptance as a full sovereign state. In 1923 the Irish Free State entered the League of Nations, and in 1924 appointed its own minister in Washington, a step no other dominion had yet taken. There followed in 1926 a bid for election to the League Council, which although not immediately successful (the Free State won admittance to the Council four years later) led to the enunciation of the principle that the dominions were full equals of the United Kingdom in the international community. In turn this paved the way for the resolution at the Imperial Conference of 1926, that all states within the British Empire were 'equal in status, in no way subordinate to one another in any aspect of their domestic or external affairs'. Thus, within five years of the Treaty, and despite a desperate armed struggle to establish the

162

supremacy of the new Irish government on its own soil, most remaining traces of British hegemony had been removed, and 'dominion status' radically redefined.

These advances were confirmed and clarified at the next Imperial Conference in 1930; and pressures generated then—again partly through Irish agitation—ended in the Statute of Westminster in 1931, empowering any dominion to repeal, unilaterally, United Kingdom legislation hitherto binding in its territory. The way was now clear for a repudiation by the Free State of any distasteful clause in the Treaty: in fact, in the Commons debate on the measure in November 1931, Churchill resisted it on this very ground. Meanwhile, the Free State had already struck a blow at the imperial structure in another vulnerable region in 1929. In accepting the ultimate jurisdiction of the Permanent Court of International Justice to determine disputes between signatory states, it repudiated the imperial principle that disputes between the United Kingdom and the dominions were domestic matters, not subject to international adjudication.

Within a decade, Cosgrave's government had established that membership of the Empire was essentially voluntary and bound the dominions to common action only to the degree to which they were prepared to bind themselves. It had also laid the foundations of an independent Irish foreign policy. This was disassociated from specific British interests, being in part neutralist and in part an expression of small states' concern for international order in a world where powers and power-blocs sought their own advantages.

De Valera, therefore, found the ball teed for him when he entered office in 1932. He felt, to say the least, no moral obligation to preserve the Treaty, and soon removed the Oath of Allegiance to the Crown, appeals to the Privy Council from Irish judicial decisions, and automatic British citizenship for Irish subjects. The British government protested that each of these repeals violated the solemn constitutional concordat of 1922. De Valera was unmoved. On the one hand, he pleaded the invalidity of the Treaty;

on the other, he could rely on the Statute of Westminster, which had undermined the British case. These early triumphs were followed by a coup in 1936, when the abdication of Edward VIII suddenly presented the Irish government with the initiative. They proceeded to delete the king from the constitution, and to employ him as the mere representative of the Irish Free State in international business, and even then only whenever the Free State was acting in concert with the other members of the Empire.

A new Irish constitution followed soon, in 1937—again it was a unilateral departure. In terms of Anglo-Irish relations the two new turns of the screw were a provision for a President, as head of state, and a change in title from Irish Free State to Ireland or, in Gaelic, Eire, with a claim to sovereignty—albeit not to be pressed immediately—over the entire island. None of this apparent brinkmanship in the 1930s was really dangerous. The basic weakness of the British position was their fixed resolve that Ireland must never leave the Empire. So long as the Irish stopped short of a direct and specific repudiation of all imperial connections, the British government would in the end find a formula to reconcile virtually any Irish innovation with its own theories of commonwealth. There was irony, bordering upon farce, in the manner in which the captive in the imperial tower dismantled so many of the confining walls that the gaoler scarcely knew what he had left.

When de Valera was elected President of the Council of the League of Nations in 1932, he also carried forward the standard of an independent Irish foreign policy. It was not that he opposed all, or even most, of the proposals that the British government endorsed. In fact, he joined the Free State with Great Britain in advocating the admission of the Soviet Union to the League, the application of sanctions against Italy in 1935, and non-intervention (as well as non-recognition of Franco) in Spain. But his basic purpose was the repudiation of force as the arbiter of international politics; and in the name of small nations, he did not spare the great powers in his addresses.

By good fortune, he was enabled in 1938 to make Irish neutralism more than a pious aspiration. According to the Anglo-Irish London Agreement of that year, the British government surrendered the three Irish naval bases that it had insisted on retaining in the Treaty of 1921. 'It was', as T.P. Coogan observes, 'possibly the only successful application of Chamberlain's appeasement policy.'[19] Perhaps Chamberlain considered that good relations with Ireland in a European war, which was already probable, were worth the price. If so, he may well, from his own standpoint, have paid too much. British possession of the bases during the Second World War might well have made Irish neutrality impossible, and forced Ireland sooner or later into the Allied camp. At any rate, Chamberlain's fateful concession completed by 1938 the process of constitutional liberation, except in that limited and shadowy region of the Crown as figurehead, where, with ultimate 're-integration' with the north to be borne in mind, it might serve to Ireland's advantage to call a halt.

Civil war

Meanwhile, in 1922 it was doubtful whether the liberation would be constitutional at all. De Valera, together with two of his six cabinet ministers, and 57 of the 121 members of the Dail, rejected the Treaty outright. He then proposed that he himself remain in office with a government composed of anti-Treatyites until 'the Irish people' determined whether or not they would surrender their Republic for a Free State. This extraordinary scheme was roughly brushed away. De Valera was voted out of power, and lost seats at the subsequent general election. All this time both sections of Sinn Fein (and especially Collins on the pro-Treaty side) had striven desperately to avoid a permanent division in the movement. It was probably a hopeless endeavour from the start; but its failure was ensured when, ten days after the election, the radical Republican wing of the IRA denied the legitimacy of the Dail and its decisions, and attempted to set up what would have been virtually a military dictatorship. The long-threatened civil war had begun at last. Once the guns spoke, no middle ground was left. De Valera, forced to choose, joined the anti-Treaty forces, carrying his Dail faction with him into the fray.

The civil war, which produced proportionately more bloodshed and destruction than the Anglo-Irish conflict of 1919–21, lasted less than a year. By May 1923 the Republicans were forced into unconditional surrender although they succeeded in dumping rather than yielding up their remaining arms. De Valera, who had set up his own rival government (replete with 'cabinet') in mid-1922, did not dismantle this immediately; it was however little more than an empty form once the Free State had established its authority. He had now to find a way out of the political dead end into which he had blundered. His most prominent difficulty was the Oath of Allegiance to the Crown required by the Treaty of all Dail members. To this was added, in March 1925, a similar requirement of a declaration of allegiance to the Irish Free State from all public servants and members of all public bodies before they could enter, or retain, office. Cosgrave's ministry, which had already begun the release of Republican prisoners, had decided that constitutional government was impossible unless the new state was accepted as a fact.

De Valera's first step back into constitutionalism was his break with the IRA in November 1925, when that body determined to act as an exclusively military organisation. Four months later, he distanced himself from even those non-military Republicans who still refused to recognise the new state or engage in political competition with the 'renegade' Cosgravites. Next, he set up a new party, Fianna Fail, and drew up a program that not merely repeated the Republican orthodoxies, but also produced various new social and economic policies. The general election held in June 1927 amply justified de Valera's return to parliamentary politics. Fianna Fail came within three seats of Cosgrave's party, which fell short, moreover, of an absolute majority in the Dail.

De Valera had still one more pit of his own digging to climb out of. He had always refused to take the Oath of Allegiance; even now his party was debarred, by its self-denying ordinance, from serving in Parliament. Cosgrave provided the means of release, by introducing a Bill to render vacant the seats of all deputies who failed to subscribe to the Oath. The subsequent crisis enabled de Valera to carry his own sea-green incorruptibles with him, when, declaring enigmatically that he signed the Oath 'in the same way that I would sign an autograph in a newspaper', he led his followers into the Chamber on 10 August 1927. Parliamentary government in the Free State had lived through its sickly infancy.

Not that early childhood was much easier than infancy for the cause of constitutionality in Ireland. The economic consequences of the Great Depression, combined with the emergence or growth of totalitarian parties all over Europe, brought the forces of violence to the fore again. By 1931, illegal drillings, shootings and intimidation by the IRA had become almost daily occurrences. Moreover, it had now a left as well as a right wing—Saor Eire, a quasi-Marxist group. Cosgrave's government responded with a harsh *Public Safety Act*, equalling or exceeding the once-familiar British coercion measures. Military courts with power to impose the death penalty; the proscription of organisations 'dangerous to the state'; and cat-and-mouse detention of IRA suspects were all legalised. Majority rule was again vindicated; but to de Valera's and not Cosgrave's benefit. At the General Election of February 1932, four months after the *Public Safety Act* had come into operation, Fianna Fail gained seventy-two seats, sufficient to place de Valera in power—at last. Since 1925 he had played his hand superbly;

and his attainment of office in 1932 (confirmed in the following year when he sought and received an overall parliamentary majority) ended the second crisis for Irish democracy.

It entered its final phase of danger almost as soon as its second ended. The threat this time was that some form or other of totalitarianism would take root. The original spur toward this development (apart, of course, from current Continental example) lay in the expectation that the change in government in 1932 would also involve a change in the character of the state. It was widely believed that former office-holders would be proscribed and persecuted for their earlier 'treason' to the Republic or else that the Cosgravites would refuse to surrender power peacefully to their enemies. The danger that the gun would return to Irish politics increased. It was an escalatory process. The Cosgrave government's stern reaction in 1931 to the re-emergence of violence bred further violence directed against itself; in turn, the Cosgravites began to take up arms, originally in self-protection. De Valera's riposte, in July 1933, of establishing an armed police and seizing firearms, frightened his political opponents still more; and fears for their defencelessness led them further along the road to force. Meanwhile, the IRA had supported de Valera's drive to power, and regarded themselves as, temporarily and conditionally at least, his allies. Thus, by 1933–34 each of the major parties in the Free State was threatened by the armed faction that supported it. It was the Treatyites who stood in the greater peril for, in September 1933, they had actually joined forces with a new militant body of the right, the National Guard (or 'Blueshirts'), which was close to, if not actually in, the current mode of European Fascism.

De Valera responded to the Blueshirts in 1934 precisely as Cosgrave had responded to IRA extravagances in 1931. He revived the *Public Safety Act.* Under its provisions, he banned a projected Blueshirt march on government buildings (shades of Mussolini's March on Rome!), and declared the National Guard a prohibited body. When the Blueshirts submitted peacefully to these decrees, the worst was over. Almost immediately afterwards the Treatyites (now Fine Gael) seized a chance to rid the party of its embarrassing protectors. The old constitutionalists had decided not to cross the Rubicon into the land of lawlessness. They returned, doubtless chastened and relieved, to mere parliamentary opposition. The Blueshirt movement did not die immediately: IRA reprisals and involvement in a species of land war (non-payment of annuities and rates) in several areas kept it fitfully alive. But after the autumn of 1934 it ceased to be, in any sense, a national danger; and gradually, sloughed off by the parliamentarians, it withered in isolation.

Ireland's equivalent of the 'left', the IRA, presented equal difficulties to Fianna Fail. But de Valera proved as skilled in office as he had been when out of power. He offered no direct assault for several years. On the contrary, he moved immediately as far towards Republican symbolism as a constitutional minister safely could, without downright repudiation of the Treaty. Each of de Valera's measures against the National Guard could, however, be turned with equal force against the extreme Republicans. The revived *Public Safety Act*, the special police and the ban on firearms were as appropriate a counter to violence on the left as on the right; and, quite apart from the machinery of repression, the long campaign against the Blueshirts had conditioned (or reconditioned) Irish public opinion to the view that the state must assert its sovereignty, come what might.

The IRA had been outflanked on both sides. The government's tone and measures were sufficiently Republican to leave only the radical fringe seriously dissatisfied with their inadequacy, while its firmness had established unassailably the authority of Parliament. From 1932 onward the IRA was sinking, in the popular estimation, from a powerful body of armed idealists on whose sufferance the government was allowed to govern to a divided body whose only common principles appeared to be an unattainable political ideal and an ineradicable faith in violence. Under pressure, the extremists began to break up in 1935, through differences over tactics, priorities and the validity of socialist values. Simultaneously, a few brutal and wanton killings by the IRA (none of them, incidentally, sanctioned by the leadership) produced a final national revulsion against the organisation. De Valera, who had used the military tribunals cautiously in 1935 to draw the teeth of the extremists, decided in June 1936 that the day of reckoning had come at last. The IRA was proscribed as an illegal body; its chief of staff was imprisoned; and its public assemblies came to an end. The third crisis of parliamentarianism was over.

One issue taken up by de Valera on his advent to power in 1932 was not however settled until 1938. This was his repudiation of the financial agreement of 1926 between the Free State and Great Britain which laid down the annual payments due to the British government for earlier land purchase advances, loans to Irish local authorities and pensions to former British administrators. The United Kingdom at once attempted to recover these monies by imposing additional duties on imports from Ireland; and the Irish government replied in kind. Nearly six years of mutually injurious tariff war ensued. The London Agreement which ended the economic conflict was financially most favourable to the Irish: £10 million was accepted by Britain as 'a final settlement' of all forms of Irish indebtedness. At least equally significant was Chamberlain's gratuitous surrender of the Irish naval bases retained in 1921. It was a victory, at least 'on points', for de Valera's celebrated obduracy. Another door was closed forever on Ireland's experiences under the Act of Union. But the hidden costs were also very large. Some at least of the terrible poverty of the Irish masses in the 1930s is attributable to the pursuit of national self-esteem in a cause of doubtful morality; and still more time and energy had been lavished on sterile political retrospective.

The Boundary Commission

The protracted conflict over sovereignty in the new state was a major factor in limiting that state's geographical extent. From a nationalist standpoint, the Boundary Commission failed to salvage anything from the wreck of 'Irish unity' in 1921. Partly because of the Irish civil war and partly also because of Cosgrave's reluctance to risk the chances of an imposed settlement, the Commission did not meet until November 1924. Altogether, two unnecessary years elapsed before its deliberations opened, and this time told steadily against the Free State's interests.

The adjudicators came to the matter with three distinct and conflicting purposes. MacNeill, the Free State representative, expected the cession of all areas reasonably contiguous to the border that contained substantial Nationalist majorities—approximately one-third of the land area of the six counties. Fisher, the Ulsterman, wanted a frontier band of solid Unionist districts, without regard to the size of the nationalist areas behind them. Feetham, the chairman, once a member of Milner's 'kindergarten' in South Africa, was also a judge, crabbed in statutory interpretation and respectful of the fait accompli. Meanwhile, MacNeill helped on the destruction of nationalist hopes by remaining in the Commission until the eleventh hour, keeping his government in ignorance of the trend of its deliberations, and then resigning precipitately when a report advocating only minor changes was on the point of publication. Cosgrave, in despair, settled for the existing boundary in a hastily concluded post-Treaty treaty in December 1925. 'Northern Ireland' was safe at last. But had the Boundary Commission represented a peril at all to the North by 1925? Even if its findings had been all that Griffith and Collins had expected, it seems doubtful whether they would—or even could— have been peacefully enforced after almost five years of independent Unionist government in the six counties.

From the start, Northern Ireland was, as a British official reported in 1938, necessarily 'a Protestant "state"', otherwise it would not have come into being'.[20] It is an open question whether it would have been quite so Protestant a 'state' were it not for the long interval between the opening of its Parliament in mid-1921 and the report of the Boundary Commission four and a half years later. The Ulster Unionists had begun at once the work of establishing a separate central administration, a separate system of local government and a separate police; this last was augmented by a body of armed all-Protestant auxiliaries, the 'B Specials'. Northern Irish Catholics (or nationalists, for the words were virtually synonomous) were grossly under-represented in— where they were not absolutely excluded from—every area within the public sphere. They themselves contributed something to this result. Initially, they refused to be involved in any way in what they regarded as not only an illegitimate authority but also one destined soon to be superseded. As their first hope, that Northern Ireland would speedily collapse, faded, they still counted on the Commission awarding large tracts of territory to the Free State. There was the further possibility that the surviving Protestant enclave would prove 'non-viable'—a vague but widely canvassed concept of the day.

In consequence, the Unionists had the field to themselves during the formative stages of the new 'Ulster'; and they systematically arranged it, so far as practicable, so as to establish Protestant monopolies as well as Protestant supremacy. They justified their actions on two grounds. First, they claimed that the nationalist community had been instructed to boycott and obstruct the political processes— the word was (as the Unionist prime minister, Craig, put it) 'No, nothing must be done to enable the Unionist government to get well-established'.[21] Second, they argued that the nationalists were, practically by definition, disloyal to the regime and therefore properly debarred from all public positions of trust and the various privileges that accompanied such responsibilities.

172

If the charges themselves were undeniable, they also reflected the anomalous nature of Northern Ireland as a separate entity. Its *raison d'être*, the preservation of the British Protestant tradition, rendered the northern Catholics, if not necessarily enemies, at least permanent malcontents within the state. Their hostility and feelings of frustration were all the greater because the new order was constructed against their interests before their last hope, the Boundary Commission, had failed them. Even in 1920 they had been heavily disadvantaged in terms of jobs, housing, urban amenities, schools and health services. By 1926 the new governmental system had deepened and entrenched the inferiority—and indeed hopelessness—of their position in many districts.

From 1926 on Protestant ascendancy was confirmed. When the Nationalist MPs (or at least some of them) at last decided to attend the Northern Ireland Parliament at Stormont, they found themselves to be a small, powerless and permanent minority. Nationalists were also an impotent minority in most county and other local bodies, often despite their constituting a majority of the population. Electoral boundaries were rigged to produce this end: Derry and Omagh were notorious instances of gerrymandering. Parallel Catholic institutions, such as schools and hospitals, suffered from their late entry into, or late attempt to reach some agreement with, the established order. Ritual celebration of Protestant triumphs and superiority confirmed Catholic alienation from a state that was virtually identified with such demonstrations; and in their turn Catholic manifestations of such alienation provided ammunition for those Unionists who demanded the unrelenting suppression of the enemy within.

Down to 1939, however, northern Protestants never escaped from a sense of insecurity and a host of fears. There were fears that they might eventually be outbred by the indigenous Catholic population. There were fears that their majority might be reduced by the incursion of immigrants from the Free State, to counter which the government introduced various restrictive measures. (How comical, in the light of these measures, that the Ulster Unionists should have struggled so hard to retain border regions where Catholics heavily predominated within their frontiers.) There were fears, especially in 1931–32, that Northern Ireland might collapse economically under the impact of the Great Depression (ruinous for Ulster's important export industries) and the burden of constant comparisons with the average incomes, standard of living, employment rates and level of social services in the remainder of the United Kingdom. The greatest of all fears was that of Protestant disunity.

The danger, in Unionist eyes, was a split along either class or internal sectarian lines, or both. It was to counter this danger (and especially the growth of a local Labour Party) rather than to disadvantage the Nationalists still further, that the Northern Ireland government abolished proportional representation for parliamentary elections at the first possible opportunity. The Depression opened up the dreaded possibility that the Catholic and Protestant unskilled workers and unemployed might join forces against oppressive capitalism. Such a junction actually took place briefly in Belfast in 1932 when the already reduced poor relief payments were cut again. Fundamentalist Protestants presented a different problem. Here the danger was, from the official standpoint, that their virulent anti-popery and Bible-based demands in education and social practice, might produce so repressive a regime as not only to alienate moderates in Ulster itself but also to draw down British and perhaps even international condemnation. The Unionist Party's answers to these various perils were single member constituencies in order to reduce the chances of breakaway Protestant candidates succeeding; the promotion of working class sections within their own organisation; reliance on the Orange Order to bind their community together; submission, especially before general elections, to extreme Protestant demands in such fields as education; and, above all, the evocation of 'the Fatherland in danger' and 'Croppy lie down' sentiments to produce a closing of the ranks.

These answers were certainly adequate for the party's easy retention of government for as long as Stormont lasted, that is until 1972. Even in their worst electoral performance, in 1925, the official Unionists won 32 of the 52 parliamentary seats and normally they carried at least 36. Yet they continued to be haunted by the spectre of Protestant division throughout the 1920s and 1930s; and their most common response was a wholesale surrender to popular Protestant prejudice and self-interest whenever the spectre seemed to loom particularly large, as it usually did before elections.

Divided Ireland

Ireland had perforce two 'economies' after 1922. Although this produced no major changes in the way either part of the divided island operated down to the outbreak of the Second World War, they inevitably drifted apart, to some extent. Whatever could be said of the Free State, it would be straining matters to speak of Northern Ireland as a distinct, let alone a 'viable' economic unit. With an area of only 5237 square miles (approx. 13 500 km²) and no major port, it was much too small to operate independently. Moreover every large economic decision that affected it was taken not in Belfast but in London, and with British interests as a whole in view. There was, however, the compensating advantage that, especially from 1931 onwards, Northern Ireland was effectively subsidised by Britain. Besides, its agriculture probably benefited significantly from the British connection, not only in terms of market access but also by support for the efforts to improve livestock strains and the guaranteed quality of farm produce.

On the other hand, unemployment in Northern Ireland was extraordinarily high, even by the British standards of

175

the 1930s. This was especially the case in the greater Belfast area where some 60 per cent of the population of Northern Ireland lived. The collapse of Belfast's export-directed industries in the Great Depression proved disastrous—and lasting, for 1938 was the worst year of all. The Northern Ireland government was virtually powerless to promote recovery by its own efforts. But Whitehall proved increasingly sympathetic towards at least the alleviation of the effects of the unemployment, while remaining blind to the systematic favour shown to the Protestant community in the management and distribution of the available resources.

For all its economic difficulties, Northern Ireland showed a net gain in population between the wars whereas the Irish Free State continued the post-Famine tradition of unbroken falls. To a much greater extent than in the six counties, economic activity in the twenty-six was still dominated by agriculture. Another post-Famine tradition, the consolidation of holdings and the migration of the 'surplus' members of farm families, also went on unabated. Such was to be the case for the first forty years of the new state's existence, and is the fundamental reason for the persistent decline in the numbers of its population down to the 1960s.

Despite the continuation of gradual consolidation, the majority of the farms in the twenty-six counties were still very small between the wars, with one-third of them below thirty acres (12 ha) in extent and most of the remainder in the 30–50 acre (12–20 ha) range. The essential change was that of ownership. By the mid-1920s the process of land purchase by the former tenants was virtually complete. It was a formal rather than a material change, not that the transference of title was of small significance. On the contrary, it was politically and psychologically of first importance. But it heralded no agricultural revolution. Farming methods and productivity remained much the same, and the structure and rhythms of rural society altered little before 1939.

This was characteristic of the Free State as a whole. At independence, it already possessed an elaborate infrastructure of public works and communications, of banks and other monetary instruments, of wholesale and retail outlets; skilled civil servants and a sophisticated administrative system; enough, if not good enough, houses and hospitals; universal primary education and literacy; and cheap, plentiful and relatively advanced secondary schools and universities. In all these respects, it was already a developed country, if not indeed 'overdeveloped'. This face of the Irish economy represented stability almost to the point of stagnation. It also provided an ironic commentary on 'breaking the connection with England'. For after independence the Irish output of manpower, professional and unskilled alike, went, not decreasingly, but increasingly to Great Britain, while the Irish government and banks continued to pursue British fiscal and economic policies at a respectful distance, and the many Irish workers who belonged to British trade unions retained their memberships.

In short, the economic response of the Irish Free State to its new situation was feeble, and the economic benefits of political independence were for a long time of small account. Between 1921 and 1959 the Irish rate of economic growth was only 1 per cent per annum, although the country's external assets remained extraordinarily large in relation to the gross national product throughout these years. Most of this money was invested in one form or another in Great Britain. Moreover, apart from one small loan in the 1920s, Ireland never borrowed abroad, although it could certainly have done so on relatively favourable terms at most stages. Thus, neither capital nor credit was used for development to any large extent before 1960. The bulk of national investment went toward the replacement or extension of the existing network of houses, roads, schools, hospitals and the like, and not into the directly productive sectors of the economy.

It would be anachronistic to condemn the first ministries in the new state for their failure to adopt the policies, or evaluate their problems in the terms that are fashionable today. Not merely did Gladstonianism still reign in treasury departments the world over; Irish independence arrived at a moment peculiarly inopportune for the economics of development. International trade was contracting, prices were falling and, as usual in these circumstances, the primary producers were worst hit of all. The fact remains, however, that constitutional autonomy produced little significant change in either the structure or the behaviour of the Irish economy in nearly four decades. In Yeats's bitter epitome:

> Parnell came down the road, he said to a cheering man:
> 'Ireland shall get her freedom and you still break stone'.

There were some attempts to strike new courses. The most ambitious and coherent came in the early years of the first de Valera regime, 1932–36. Alternative markets to the United Kingdom were sought for Irish agricultural exports, while protective tariffs were simultaneously set up to enable native industries to develop. Neither policy was successful, as might indeed have been predicted, for the government had been moved by political rather than economic considerations. First, the idea of national self-sufficiency, with the corollary of protection, had come to be accepted as a mark of doctrinal purity among Irish nationalists. More specifically, the economic war with Great Britain practically forced de Valera's government to attempt to develop new export markets and new manufacturing industries at home.

Again, it was the worst of times for such ventures. Even had international circumstances been favourable, success was unlikely, for de Valera's experiments in the 1930s represented frontal assaults, at once crude and puny, upon a very powerful economic force—the long-established dependence of a hinterland upon a developed centre for its markets and supplies. De Valera himself was as lacking in acquisitive and commercial instincts as in economic sophistication. His vision of Ireland free was of a land of small farms, modest incomes and simple lives.

The Ireland we dreamed of [he once said] would be the home of a people who valued material wealth only as the basis of right living, of a people who were satisfied with frugal comfort and devoted their leisure to the things of the spirit . . . It would, in a word, be the home of people living the life that God desires that man should live.[25]

There was no room for economic miracles in this amalgam of monastic and arcadian ideals.

The impact of World War II

The Thucydidean dictum that war changes everything had mixed application in Ireland when Europe burst into armed conflict once again. Although it might well be applied to Northern Ireland both during and after the Second World War, it was far from apparent in Eire between 1939 and 1945. Instead, war seemed to sustain the status quo there for perhaps a decade. De Valera had prepared carefully for the Armageddon. As President of the League of Nations in 1938, he became painfully certain of the coming devastation, and was quick to declare his neutrality in advance. But, having rendered neutrality practicable in 1938 by securing the Irish naval bases hitherto in British hands, he also made it clear that Eire would serve British interests to any reasonable limit. Three months before the invasion of Poland, he assured Great Britain that Irish territory would never be used for hostile actions. As he had further (if tacitly) promised, Eire's neutrality was in fact one-sided. The German forces, economy, and propaganda and espionage apparatus did not enjoy the advantages and opportunities that de Valera afforded their British counterparts. Germany quietly accepted this 'special relationship'. Presumably it considered (as presumably de Valera had calculated that it would) that the denial of the use of Irish Atlantic ports to Great Britain constituted a sufficient compensation.

At any rate, Eire, unscathed, contributed heavily to the war effort of her hereditary foe. Directly, Britain was supported by 30 000 Irish recruits in her armed services, and by a very much larger number of Irish men and women in her work force; by food supplied; and by mounting unspent sterling balances. Indirectly, the Irish neutrality laws, as they were actually applied, worked decidedly in favour of Great Britain. It was only natural that the British government, especially in the phases following the fall of France and preceding the invasion of 1944, should have been tempted to end some of its difficulties by seizing Eire, and in particular her western and southern ports, by force of arms. Once more de Valera had calculated nicely. The balance of advantage, even for a Great Britain under pressure, lay in amicable relations between the islands.

Doubtless, it was much to survive intact in 1939–45. But the domestic costs of Irish neutrality were considerable. The war reinforced what was by now a near-stagnant state of politics and society. The condition reached in the political system by the mid-1930s was simply perpetuated. The two main parties, deriving from the Treaty division, engrossed 70 to 80 per cent of the parliamentary representation, with de Valera always in power, either close to or actually enjoying an absolute majority in the Dail. By 1939 Fianna Fail seemed, temporarily at least, to have exhausted its creative purposes. The new constitutional system had been established; Republican symbolism had been imposed up to the level that de Valera considered prudent in the light of other national interests; the very modest measures of social reform, which were consequential on the economic war and the party's dependence upon workers' and small farmers' votes, had been carried through with a decided air of finality; and the limitations of protectionist industrialism of the old Sinn Fein variety had been thoroughly exposed. But the extinct volcanoes of 1939 were not to be disturbed for nine years more.

The war goes far to explain this protracted retention of office after Fianna Fail's positive program had petered out, and the government's functions became increasingly executive. How dangerous it might be to disturb de Valera's power upon the very brink of the abyss! An important side-effect, however, was the intensification of the national acquiescence in immobility. Moreover, in the Second World War, unlike the First, the check on emigration to North America had no significant effect on Irish political or social development. Emigration to the USA had been small since 1920. On this occasion the British war factories and service industries possessed an insatiable appetite for Irish labour. Thus potential discontents dispersed while fears of change remained specific. Meanwhile the bleakness and meanness of material life in wartime—even in an island of peace— were matched by emotional and intellectual impoverishment. In a society already small, inward-looking and self-absorbed, the general, compulsory and unheroic isolation comfirmed all that was static or retrogressive in its composition. It was not easy to recover from these deprivations.

From the beginning of the war, Northern Ireland's path diverged sharply from that of Eire. Conscription was not imposed there, but otherwise the province was practically on a par with Britain. It too was fully committed to the war effort, with a concomitant increase in both agricultural and industrial employment. Belfast, now a centre of aircraft as well as ship production, was bombed heavily several times in 1941—leading, incidentally, to a temporary warming of north-south relations as rescue and relief services from Eire poured across the border to help their stricken neighbours. Derry and Lough Foyle provided vital bases in the air and sea struggle for command of the North Atlantic. The whole province was knitted into the European conflict from first to last, in a sharp contrast to Eire's isolation.

This internationalisation was accentuated by the presence of American troops in large numbers, especially during 1943 and 1944. The United States was impatient at the military costs of de Valera's neutrality, and there is some reason to believe that it was restrained from taking over Eire by force only by Britain's influence. However that may have been, the contrast between the two parts of Ireland naturally coloured American and other belligerents' attitudes. Stormont stood high in the esteem of the victorious Allied powers in 1945; and Unionists were triumphant in what seemed to them the ultimate vindication of their loyalism. Eire, on the contrary, had lost something of the sympathy and reflex support that it customarily enjoyed in the United States and even some quarters of the Commonwealth.

Not only did the war enlarge the horizons, revive the economy and raise the confidence of Northern Ireland but also it led indirectly to profound changes in its social order. British wartime and postwar legislation designed to produce a brave new world at home—the *Education Act* of 1944, the *Family Allowance Act* of 1945, the *National Insurance*, *National Health* and *Public Health Acts* of 1946 and the *National Assistance Act* of 1948—either applied directly to or had counterparts for Northern Ireland. Cumulatively, they advanced the province's system of social security beyond what the twenty six counties could then contemplate. The gap between north and south was enlarged; and it was the Catholics of Northern Ireland, as the neediest section of the population, who gained most materially. The immediate advantages—and not least the immediate political advantages—of all this for the Ulster Unionists is obvious, even if the seeds of great future trouble for them were also being sown. All told, the war seemed to have augmented and secured their power, and it was to be many a day before they were at last awakened to a realisation of its long term inimical effects.

9

Epilogue: From 1945

The Republic

The first of the major changes of the past half-century or so was the Dail's passage of the *Republic of Ireland Act* of 1949 which swept the twenty-six counties out of the Commonwealth. In some respects, this was an accidental stroke. Fianna Fail, weighed down by maladministration and the onset of the postwar depression, lost the general election of 1948; and the replacement government, a rainbow coalition of various other parties, large and small, conservative and radical, opened the way to reckless ventures as the price to be paid for so heterogeneous a combination. It is doubtful if more than one-tenth of the membership of the new Dail wished to take the leap to an openly declared Republic at that stage, but the circumstances were propitious for a determined minority to force this through. As a bizarre consequence, the old Treatyites, although numerically dominant in the Coalition Government, were placed at the head of the Republican column, dragging the chagrined but helpless de Valera and his party in their train.

It was not love of the British Commonwealth per se that explains the reluctance with which Fianna Fail and Fine Gael alike severed the last ties. It was fear of the economic and social consequences. Not only was Anglo-Irish trade

The Irish Review

THE ONLY IRISH NEWSPAPER IN AUSTRALIA   THE TRUTH ABOUT IRELAND

Vol. 23. No. 2.   Registered at the G.P.O., Melbourne, for Transmission by Post as a Newspaper.   MELBOURNE, FEBRUARY, 1954.   Price 6d.

Australia not Sending Ambassador to Ireland

Difficulty Over Letters of Credence

Letters of credence which had been proposed for the appointment of Mr. Paul McGuire as Ambassador to Ireland had contained a phrase which might have thrown doubt on the validity of the Queen's title as "Queen of the United Kingdom and Northern Ireland."

The Minister for External Affairs (Mr. Casey) stated this at Canberra on 17 January in elaborating on the reasons for the Australian Government's decision not to proceed with the appointment.

He said neither the Australian Government, nor he, himself, would consider asking the Queen to do something in her capacity of Queen of Australia which would embarrass her in her capacity as Queen of the United Kingdom and Northern Ireland.

Therefore, it had been impossible for Australia to ask the Queen to sign letters of credence for Mr. McGuire, addressed to "The President of Ireland," as the Government of the Republic of Ireland had insisted.

Mr. Casey said he greatly regretted the situation which had arisen because of the close ties between Ireland and Australia and the contributions made to the development of Australia by persons of Irish extraction.

In Dublin, the Minister of External Affairs (Mr. Aiken) said that he had been informed by the Australian Minister for External Affairs that the Australian Government had decided not to proceed with the appointment of Mr. Dominic Paul McGuire as Ambassador at Dublin.

"The difficulty arose," said Mr. Aiken, "from inability to find agreement upon the manner in which Mr. McGuire's Letters of Credence should be addressed. Every effort had been made to reach agreement, but unfortunately without success. When the Australian Government sought the Irish Government's assent to Mr. McGuire's nomination in

More Employment at Forestry

Fresh planting of forests in Ireland was, last year, slightly over the target of 12,500 acres and was spread over 119 forests. For the current year the immediate target is 15,000 acres in new forest. The area requiring thinning will increase steadily towards 20,000 acres a year over the next 10 to 15 years. During 1952-53 forestry work employed the biggest labour force ever and the further development plans will need a 15 per cent. labour-force increase.

The Australian Government had decided not to proceed with the appointment of Mr. Paul McGuire, O.B.E., as Ambassador to Ireland. Announcing this decision, the Minister of External Affairs (Mr. Casey) said that Letters of Credence which had been proposed had contained a phrase which might have thrown doubt on the validity of the Queen's title as "Queen of the United Kingdom and Northern Ireland." In a statement issued in Dublin, the Irish Minister of External Affairs (Mr. Aiken) pointed out that when the Australian Government sought the Irish Government's assent to Mr. McGuire's nomination, the Irish Ambassador (Dr. Kiernan) indicated that the Letters of Credence should be addressed to the President in his constitutional title, President of Ireland. Subsequently, the Australian Government announced Mr. McGuire's appointment.

April, 1953," Mr. Aiken went on, "the Irish Ambassador, Dr. Kiernan, called at the Department of External Affairs in Canberra. He took occasion to point out that the Letters of Credence should be addressed to the President in his constitutional title, President of Ireland."

The Irish Government gave their assent to Mr. McGuire's nomination and subsequently the Australian Government announced his appointment.

Some weeks after the announcement, however, the Australian Government raised objections to having the Letters of Credence addressed to the President of Ireland, and since then, notwithstanding many exchanges of views, no acceptable solution had been found.

PAUL McGUIRE

Mr. Aiken was asked by the Diplomatic Correspondent of the Irish News

withdrawal of the Irish Ambassador at Canberra. "It is not our intention to withdraw him," the Minister replied, "as in this case no constitutional difficulty has arisen."

Asked what effect the decision was likely to have on Australian representation in Dublin, Mr. Aiken replied, "So far as the Irish Government is concerned, none."

Asked if he had any comments on Mr. Casey's statement of 17th January, Mr. Aiken said:

"It would serve no useful purpose to enter into a controversy on our non-acceptance of an Australian Ambassador on the terms suggested by the Australian Government.

"I must repeat, however, that before the Irish Government assented to the nomi-

Agency whether the Australian decision not to proceed with the appointment of Mr. McGuire would involve the

nation of Mr. McGuire as Ambassador and before his appointment was announced in Canberra the Australian Government were officially notified that the Letters of Credence should be addressed in accordance with the normal practice to the President of Ireland.

"In the case of Britain which is keeping Ireland partitioned against the wishes of the majority of the Irish people, it was decided for the peaceful solution of that issue that diplomatic relations should be maintained at the highest level. Such (Continued on page 4)

Most Brilliant Irishman of His Generation

TRIBUTE TO TOM KETTLE, PATRIOT AND POET

BY VINCENT RUE
in
"Irish Press"

One of my fellow students at Law Lectures in King's Inns was Tom Kettle, and my personal friendship with him has always remained for me a cherished memory.

We began with what I may call a political bond in that we both came of Parnellite families, his father being a distinguished supporter of the great Irish leader.

Tom Kettle was the most brilliant Irishman of his generation—a many-sided genius, Poet, orator, statesman, humanitarian, patriot, he towered above all his contemporaries. To which of these forms of human endeavour would he turn his amazing gifts? None could tell for indeed he was an enigma even to himself.

THEIR NAMES LIVE.

It was said of Yeats that if he had never written anything but the sonnet, "The Lake Isle of Innisfree," his name would live. Equally true it is of Kettle that if he had never written anything but his inspired sonnet to his baby daughter. "Betty the gift of God," his name as a poet would live. It was written in the field before Guillemont, Somme,

and is dated 4th September, 1916, two days before the battle of Guillemont, and five days before the battle of Guinchy where he was killed in action. By permission, I quote the sonnet here:—

In wiser days, my darling rosebud blown
To beauty proud as was your mother's prime,
In that desired, delayed, incredible time,
You'll ask why I abandoned you, my own,
And the dear heart that was your baby throne,
To dice with death. And oh! they'll give you rhyme
And reason: Some will call the thing sublime,
And some decry it in a knowing tone.
So here while the mad guns curse overhead,
And fired men sigh with mud for couch and floor,
Know that we fools, now with the foolish dead,
Died not for flag, nor King,
nor Emperor,
But for a dream, born in a herdsman's shed,

And for the secret Scripture of the poor.

An officer who fought with him at the battle of Guillemont told Mrs. Kettle that her husband seemed to have a charmed life. In a bitter struggle to drive the enemy from a redoubt, the gallant Dublin Fusiliers, assailed on both sides, drove the Germans back, and, counter-attacking, drove them from the field. In one of his letters home he said: "Nor did I ever think that the valour of simple men could be quite so beautiful as that of my Dublin Fusiliers." He fell in the bloody battle of Guinchy on the 9th September when leading his "Dublins" in a crashing bayonet charge, which swept the Germans before it.

For all too brief a time he sat in the House of Commons where his oratory, his flashing wit and humour and his broad humanism established him as an outstanding personality. He left the House in disgust at the betrayal of the Home Rule cause by the Liberal Party, a betrayal which led in the course of avenging history to the

eclipse of at once great party.

DEFEATED HOPES

He had previsioned the situation in which a self-governing Ireland with a Parliament for all Ireland would take its place in a United Commonwealth; but he saw his prevision dashed by the malignant anti-Irish forces, Liberal and Conservative alike, of English politics.

John Redmond, the leader of the Irish Party, reunited after the disastrous split, had accepted Asquith's Home Rule Bill, but he opposed the exclusion from the Bill of any part of the province of Ulster. He advised the Irish people to enter the war which they were told was being fought for the freedom of small nations. So bitterly anti-Irish were the English war lords, that they discouraged the enlistment of Irishmen in the army. Even John Redmond's son, William Archer Redmond was at first refused a commission. The new party of Sinn Fein, growing in strength every day, denounced Redmond's policy, and swept Redmond's party out of Parliament when the war had ended.

(Continued on page 4)

Article 2 of the new Irish Constitution of 1937 claimed jurisdiction over the entire island. Article 3 however, suspended this claim, so far as Northern Ireland was concerned, pending national 're-integration'. Australia's constitutional 'scruples' were not shared by other countries.

paramount in Eire's economy, but also the Irish pound was tied to sterling, numerous Irish institutions (from professional organisations to trade unions) were still branches of British parent bodies, hundreds of thousands of Irish nationals were residents of Great Britain, and cross-channel emigration and traffic were integral to the current workings of Irish society. In the event, thanks in no small part to Australian influence in the form of H. V. Evatt's intervention, Eire paid no significant material price for its repudiation of the Commonwealth. The British counterpart of the Irish statute, the *Ireland Act* of 1949, happily left the new Republic all the advantages of the old relationship. Indeed, the Irish continued to be dealt with by the Commonwealth Relations (and not the Foreign) Office, and were invested in Great Britain with the same rights and obligations as citizens of the United Kingdom. As in 1939–45, the British government did not, in the end, allow wounded self-esteem or old habits of thought to override their judgment of the balance of advantage. Curiously enough, it was Australia that later exacted a penalty when it excluded the citizens of the Republic of Ireland (as Eire had now become) from the operation of its assisted migration scheme.

The British 1949 Act had also to reassure the Ulster Unionists. Accordingly, it solemnly declared that Northern Ireland should never leave the United Kingdom unless voluntarily and on its own initiative. The formal final surrender by the imperial Parliament of its theoretical right to dispose of north-eastern Ireland was important. It seemed to close the last—if most unpromising—avenue of hope for the constitutional nationalists, to shut out all prospect of reaching an accommodation on the north.

To Protestant Ulster, some association with the British Crown was, as it then appeared, the one eternal and indispensable guarantee. It was doubtless with Irish unity in view that de Valera, almost from the outset of his political career, had striven to distinguish those symbols of British authority that did not detract from Irish independence from

185

those that did. Now wanton boys had torn down his delicate constitutional construction. As if this were not enough, the Coalition Government embarked concurrently (1949–50) on a strident, futile and, in many cases, disingenuous 'anti-partition' campaign. This was conducted at once tediously and noisily in the new Council of Europe, as well as at home and elsewhere abroad. Given the temper and preoccupations of postwar Europe and the reinforced constitutional bulwarks of the Northern Ireland parliament, it would be difficult to imagine a line of conduct less likely to achieve the professed object of the government, namely, to draw back the six lost counties to the Irish fold.

The political pattern of the immediate postwar years continued into the early 1950s. Recovery of the 'lost' counties remained a leading feature of debate; the IRA staged a remarkable if short-lived revival, now centred on the extension of the Republic over the entire island; and the second Coalition Government (1954–57) actually fell from power because it was defeated on a motion deploring its lack of an activist policy towards partition. During his later postwar spells of office, 1951–54 and 1957–59, de Valera too placed heavy emphasis upon the Northern Ireland question. Irish unity was as much as ever his King Charles's head, dearer even than the restoration of the Irish language.

De Valera's replacement as leader of Fianna Fail by Sean Lemass in 1959 certainly signalled the end of an era. Even before then, like the first breath of spring, there were indications that the old order in Irish politics was about to change. One harbinger was the dignity and circumspection manifested by the Irish delegates newly admitted to the United Nations in 1956, a joyous contrast to the conduct of the first representatives at the Council of Europe seven years before. But while it was much to behave fitly as citizens of the world, it was a great deal more to attempt to wrest the economy at home from the slow decline in which it had seemed fixed since 1954, if not in fact from the very inauguration of the new state; and this is what the second

Coalition showed signs of doing in its later days. The establishment of an Industrial Development Authority and the first moves toward national economic planning undertaken by the Coalition Government marked the beginning of a new age.

Not until de Valera, the very epitome of abstract Anglocentric politics, quitted the stage in 1959 was this fully apparent. But from the outset of the 1960s the Republic was increasingly absorbed in contemporary concerns; 1916, the Treaty, the fratricide seemed dying issues. Perhaps, it then seemed, they would rise again only as history, and no longer as daily torments. Perhaps Arthur Griffith's terrible questions in the Treaty debates, 'Is there to be no living Irish nation? Is the Irish nation to be the dead past or the prophetic future?' would not need to be asked again. It is one thing, however, to lay ghosts at home; another, to prevent their emigration. One can still be haunted from across a border. No more than the British rhetoric and stances of several centuries, did the rhetoric and stances of the south for fifty years cease to bear bitter fruit because they had largely withered where first they flowered.

Northern Ireland

When the second premier of Northern Ireland, Lord Brookeborough (formerly Sir Basil Brooke) retired in 1963 after twenty-three years in office, he had, it seemed, much reason for self-congratulation. The Ulster Unionist Party remained impregnably in control of government, with two-thirds of the parliamentary representation at Stormont, even after a 'poor' performance in the general election of 1962. The province as a whole, by grace of heavy subsidies from Westminster, enjoyed near-parity with Great Britain in terms of social securities and benefits, as well as medical and educational advances. By the 1950s, it had already far outstripped what the Republic could provide under any of these heads. It is true that unemployment remained high

187

by British standards, three or four times as high as the United Kingdom average—and considerably above even that if the Catholic minority is regarded as a separate entity. On the other hand, unemployment and its offspring emigration were still greater in the Republic in the years 1945–63.

On the greatest matter of all, Irish unity, not only had Northern Ireland received out of the blue a cast-iron reaffirmation of its independence in the *Ireland Act* of 1949, but also the recent IRA campaign of 1957–62, directed mainly at public buildings and installations, had petered out ingloriously. 'Attacks', as it was later reported with some complacency, 'were largely limited to sporadic incursions by small isolated parties who crossed the border for a short distance and returned immediately to Irish Republic territory'.[23] Moreover, the IRA offensive had failed to arouse significant support or even sympathy from the main body of northern Catholics, while the government of the Republic had sealed its fate by the ruthless 'detention' of suspected members. A final source of satisfaction for the Ulster Unionists was Lemass's offer, soon after he had become Taoiseach (Prime Minister) in 1959, of de facto recognition of Northern Ireland, and his efforts to promote cooperation, in economic concerns at least, between the two parts of the divided island.

If, however, Unionist Ulster never seemed steadier and more serene than in the early 1960s, the appearances were deceptive. First, despite its outward calm, the Protestant majority was both outraged and rendered insecure once more by the long series of IRA attacks upon the infrastructure of 'their' state. In hindsight, it is apparent that a strong backlash was building up. From an IRA perspective, little though the organisation realised it at the time, it had in fact taken a first step towards the destabilisation of the regime. It is significant that it was during 1957–62 that the Reverend Ian Paisley emerged as a leader of the radical Loyalists and—shades of the eighteenth century Oakboys and Defenders!—that the first modern Protestant terrorist groups were formed, more or less as a facsimile of the IRA.

Second, the Protestant majority failed to appreciate, let alone reciprocate, the general refusal of the northern Catholics to become involved in the IRA offensive, even though this was probably the most remarkable and important feature of the entire episode. Such insensitivity was symptomatic of the unaltered Unionist mindset and blindness to the potentialities opened up by the postwar social changes. The 'not-an-inch' mentality still predominated where it mattered most, in the actions and inaction of the Northern Ireland government. This had been apparent since 1945. Even in the application of the social reforms of the British Labour government of 1945–51, the Unionist administration had attempted to minimise the benefits to its Catholic citizens. More than two decades were to pass, for instance, before such Catholic institutions as hospitals managed by religious orders or the orders' voluntary grammar schools were placed on an equal footing with their Protestant counterparts as recipients of public funds. Similarly, Stormont tried later to weight the system of children's allowances in favour of small as against large families—in other words, in favour of Protestant as against Catholic. The supremacist attitude was maintained even in the field of symbols. The *Flags and Emblems Act* of 1954 declared the Union Jack protected but rendered all other signs and banners liable to police prohibition.

The most systematic means of maintaining the supremacy of Protestants was their continued control of the police forces, which moreover enjoyed extraordinarily wide powers and discretions; their continued domination of local government, often by ward-rigging and the enfranchisement of property rather than persons; their use of office, provincial and local alike, to ensure that the lion's share of public employment went to their co-religionists; and their allocations of council housing. As David Harkness observes, 'local government and public housing . . . [were] mechanisms in unionist hands with which to combat the higher Catholic birthrate, by ensuring Catholic emigration',[24] while the near-monopoly of the forces of order flowed from the very 'raison d'etre of the state, which was Protestant predominance'.[25] In none of these fields had the Unionists relaxed their grip to any material degree even twenty years after Second World War had ended.

Thus, neither Catholic alienation nor the endless Protestant quest for security had much abated by the time that civil rights movements and student protest began to sweep across the Western world. It is oversimplifying things, but not too greatly, to place the starting date of the present 'Troubles' in Northern Ireland at the formation of the Northern Ireland Civil Rights Association in 1967. The Association's main aims, 'one man one vote' in local government and the guiding principle of need rather than religious affiliation in the apportioning of public goods and especially housing, were tame and conventional enough by international standards. But the Northern Ireland context transformed them in the eyes of many Protestants into threats to the very existence of the regime. Even the Association's studied show of moderation—its eschewing of traditional political and constitutional objectives—took on a sinister appearance for the ultra-Loyalists, who saw it as an insidious device to break up Protestant solidarity by presenting the organisation as a non-sectarian, all-embracing front.

From then on, the fatal cycle with which the world has become painfully familiar over the past quarter-century was set in motion. The protest marches and 'occupations' characteristic of all the civil rights movements of the day met with violent resistance from Protestant extremists, and ultimately police violence directed increasingly at Catholic communities. This, in the new era of sensationalist and almost instant television reporting, soon reached such a pitch of armed assault and counter-assault (accompanied by the first bombs, actually planted by Unionists in the hope that the IRA would be held responsible) that in August 1969 the British Army was sent in, in considerable numbers, to constitute a peace-keeping force. Initially, the Army acted in effect as defenders of the Catholic population. It was the Catholics who were most at risk; they even lacked their customary self-appointed 'guardians', for the IRA was still struggling to reconstitute itself as a fighting unit.

The early Catholic–Army rapport was gradually reversed. The military and Northern Ireland police leaderships had to work together, and the traditional Unionist attitudes towards the issue of law and order prevailed eventually over the ideal of absolute neutrality. The IRA at last took the field during 1970—thereby evoking and provoking further Loyalist counterparts. Their attempt to establish 'no-go' (or entirely self-governing and self-defending) areas in the Catholic city ghettoes was anathema to the Army, which saw itself as the only legitimate armed force in the province, with the sole right and duty to deploy that force throughout the jurisdiction. In combination, these factors produced such an about turn in feeling during 1970 that the Army came to be regarded as an instrument of oppression by the Catholic masses, and the traditional Republican images of armed occupation began to prevail again. Concurrently, shootings and bombings, aimed partly at armed opponents, partly at people at random, and partly at property and public works, became almost daily occurrences in late 1970 and 1971.

The reform program insisted on by the British government, in an effort to undercut the traditional Catholic grievances, proceeded too slowly (not necessarily from malignancy or dissension) to influence Catholic sentiment at once, but too quickly for the Unionist Party to hold together. It was apparent as early as 1969 that Unionists were to be divided—and roughly in the proportion of half-and-half—on the issue of making any concessions whatever to their hereditary foes, even where these were demanded by Great Britain. In 1971 this split was rendered formal when Paisley set up the Democratic Unionist Party in opposition to the official Unionists, thus crystallising a key element in the intractability of the northern problem. 'It is', as J.H. Whyte concludes, 'because Protestant distrusts Protestant, not just because Protestant distrusts Catholic that the Ulster conflict is so intense'.[26] Of course there was no homogeneity of view on either side of the Unionist divide. Opinion ranged from advocates of the secularisation of northern politics at one extreme of the Unionist ranks to fellow-travelling with the Protestant paramilitarists at the other. It is also true that at moments of very great pressure the Protestant front temporarily re-formed. But overall, for the past quarter of a century, right-wing Protestant fears of being sold out by their weaker-kneed brethren have so far bedevilled every search for a peaceful outcome.

Later in 1971 however the situation was re-polarised, and was to remain in more or less that state for a considerable time. The rise in violence up to August of that year, with bombings (to say nothing of other armed attacks and counterattacks) averaging about two a day, prepared the way for a desperate decision—the introduction of internment without trial. This was a brand thrust into a power-keg in the current conditions of high tension, in particular as it was only Catholics who were arrested, and only Catholics who were tortured in the course of 'interrogation', and in 240 cases imprisoned indefinitely. The three main consequences of internment were a solidification of the bulk of the northern Catholic population in outraged protest, and of the bulk of Protestant population in satisfaction and relief; an apparent identification of British Army and Ulster Unionist interests and strategy; and a terrifying increase in the killings and destruction. As against thirty deaths by violence up to 9 August 1971, 143 took place in the remaining twenty weeks of the year.

The crisis deepened in early 1972. On the one hand, British paratroopers shot thirteen marchers dead during an unauthorised nationalist march in Derry; and with that the tension in the Bogside mounted almost intolerably. As Seamus Heaney's *Casualty* puts it,

> He was blown to bits
> Out drinking in a curfew
> Others obeyed, three nights
> After they shot dead
> The thirteen men in Derry
> PARAS THIRTEEN, the walls said,
> BOGSIDE NIL. That Wednesday
> Everybody held
> His breath and trembled.

On the other hand, Protestant extremism fell into fear and anger once again and set up, with startling immediate success, an umbrella counter-movement, Vanguard, to embrace all 'traditionalist' Unionists alarmed by the 'weakness' of their own Stormont government. Again the unexpected happened. On 24 March 1972, the British Prime Minister, Edward Heath, announced the suspension of that government, the removal of the control of security from Belfast to London, and the appointment of a Secretary of State for Northern Ireland, with ultimate powers over the administration of the province. The knot had become Gordian in British eyes: the temptation to cut it in exasperation by imposing direct rule—after nearly half-a-century of nearneglect—proved irresistible. It was, moreover, a seeming season of new beginnings. Both the United Kingdom and the Irish Republic were about to become members of the European Community at long last.

Direct rule has proved easier to assume than abandon. The original British purpose—if that is not too strong a word for what was largely impulsive action at the time—was to substitute 'community government' for one-party rule and to recognise in some formal fashion that the Irish Republic had a legitimate interest in the entire affair. Such a recognition was meant to assuage the Republic's frustration at its sense of impotence since its sensible but humiliating denial of active intervention in 1969. It was also intended to reassure northern Catholics by providing them with a sort of shadowy protector in the background. There was the further hope that the south would be drawn into regarding and treating the IRA as a common problem, to be solved by joint security measures, as had been more or less the case in the late 1950s. Although both Dublin and the new Social Democratic and Labor Party (the party, substantially, of the moderate Catholics of the north) welcomed the Heath initiative as a distinct gleam on the horizon, it did not in the event presage peace. Rather was it the first in a long succession of false dawns.

Since 1972, there have been repeated new departures in Northern Ireland, although, in many respects, the more things changed the more they remained the same. As one might expect, it was the first of the departures that seemed the most promising, until very recently. In 1973, the British government decided to set up a new assembly, with circumscribed but by no means negligible domestic responsibilities, in the north. This time not only was the mode of election to be proportional representation but also the offices were to be shared between the parties. Although the resultant administration, which took up the reins of government on 1 January 1974, contained a majority of Unionists, four members of the SDLP—wonder of wonders—were also appointed ministers. Thereby the adherence of the bulk of the Catholic population was, at least temporarily, secured.

Within five months, however, this 'new departure' had been snuffed out by the militant ultra-Loyalists, who used Protestant trade unionism to paralyse the province by strikes in order to compel the British government (Labour had recently replaced the Conservatives in office) to abandon its constitutional experiment. That government duly, indeed quite quickly, caved in. Direct rule was reimposed; and despite a succession of fresh expedients—the Northern Ireland Convention of 1975–76, the All-Ireland Forum of 1983, the Hillsborough Anglo-Irish Agreement of 1985 and

194

all the later initiatives launched from one quarter or another—despite even the IRA ceasefire of 31 August 1994, direct rule still remains the order of the day. The Ulster question has not yet changed in many of its essentials since 1972. Protestants still fear almost any move lest it prove a step on the way to ultimate subjection to an alien, abhorrent, 'Catholic' and 'Gaelic' culture. The rejection of abortion (1983) and divorce (1985) in referenda in the Irish Republic was grist—as if any more were needed—to this particular mill. The IRA may have stowed away its Armalites and explosives, but it did so while it was still a seemingly indestructible terrorist and guerrilla force; and we must not forget that it was always this destructive potential that ensured both Loyalist counterparts and military response. Nor should we forget that none of the hitherto insurmountable ideological and sectarian obstacles to a negotiated settlement has yet been conjured out of existence. As the hero of Joyce's *Portrait*, meant to personify the future Irelands, said, 'History is a nightmare from which I am trying to awake'.

Against this grudging catalogue of gloom may be set the fact that all parties in, or involved in the north have spent the past quarter of a century in an especially hard school of experience. All the world over, and in the past as well as the present, such long, cruel experiences as Northern Ireland's have led ultimately to attempts at fresh beginnings upon new bases. When exhaustion ended the Thirty Years War at last, the very causes that had done most to set it off had long before been laid aside in favour of political necessity. Moreover, Ireland itself has a history of time's accommodations and of outlooks being transformed generationally as well as a history of intransigence and deadly dogma. The Irish past provides not merely suits of armour but also irrepressible hopes and the promise of recurrent springs. It may well be—and certainly, well may it be—that 1994 will prove the mark of the opening of an

195

era that gradually leaves behind, as obsolete, the hereditary, inveterate rigidities.

Years may have to pass before this is clear, at any rate, in the historian's long, cold calculation. But already there can be no doubt, I believe, that the British about turn of 1972 represented a most profound if still not fully explicated change. The suspension of Stormont resembled, in reverse, the Act of Union of 1801. For although Northern Ireland attained 'Home Rule' in 1921, this did not happen because it was positively desired by any party. It happened because it seemed the most effective way, in the circumstances of the day, of maintaining the Act of Union, substantially, in at least six of the thirty-two counties of Ireland. So, paradoxically, the inauguration of a system of indirect rule in Northern Ireland in 1921 really signified the confirmation of the British connection. By a corresponding paradox, the establishment of direct rule almost fifty-one years later really signified the weakening, and perhaps ultimately the dissolution, of the tie between Great Britain and 'Ulster'. It is true that, at the time, full political integration between the two was said to be one of the alternative future courses. Even at the moment of Stormont's suspension, this seemed improbable; and every later twist and turn of events in the north has rendered such an outcome still more unlikely.

Both 1801 and 1972 represented the clear end of one era in the Anglo-Irish relationship, accompanied by unpredictability as to what would follow. Perhaps the most striking single feature of the British preconsideration of constitutional union in the 1790s and of direct rule in the 1970s was absorption in the immediate. Each stroke was seen as cutting ruthlessly through a hopeless tangle. But each was also undertaken without any really determined strategy. For example, whether a separate Irish executive should be maintained under the Union did not so much as cross the mind of any member of a British Cabinet until well after the Act itself was passed. The Irish substate of the nineteenth century, so critical to the shape and development of the Irish question down to 1920, was never planned; it just never—so to say—unhappened.

Correspondingly, the logical corollary of the establishment of a power-sharing assembly in Northern Ireland in 1974, as the first stage of British disengagement in Ulster, was to support that assembly by all the instruments of power in the hands of the British government. But this was forgotten or foresworn at the first manifestation, within a few months of the inauguration of mixed local rule, of serious Ulster Protestant resistance to the experiment. The strategy of 1972 was never really put to the test. Once it encountered a major, though quite predictable, obstacle, British policy veered away. Let us hope that the curriculum of the hard school of experience has included some history lessons.

'Great leaps forward'

For the Republic, too, 1972 was a fateful date for it was in that year that it decided, by a huge majority at a national referendum, to join the European Economic Community. The defeated minority had urged that such membership would detract from a hard-won and as yet uncompleted independence, and further erode Ireland's distinctive culture. Generally, such arguments fell on deaf ears. The economic gains for what would be the poorest and most agrarian member of the Community, if the Republic joined, were much too obvious for the issue to be in doubt. And over and above material considerations, there was the widespread feeling that the Republic would move closer to genuine international parity with the United Kingdom in such a body, where all members were in certain important respects constitutional equals at the least. Moreover, Irish nationalists had long identified themselves historically with three of the six founding members of the Community, France, Belgium and Italy, in each of which Irish seminaries or colleges had flourished in the seventeenth and eighteenth

197

centuries. The sentiment was especially strong in the case of France, Ireland's traditional ally and support, according to schoolbook history, from the 1680s to the 1880s and even later. Paradoxically, the Continental links had acted as an assurance of separate identity for almost 300 years.

Nevertheless, it was the economic motive that predominated in the choice. This symbolised the change that had overtaken the Republic's politics at the end of the 1950s, when the traditional issues of more or less abstract nationalism began to give way to those of national survival and prosperity. The first postwar decade had been one of depression relieved only by the increasing flight of the supposed 'surplus' population. Annual economic growth fell below 1 per cent. The relatively large national monetary assets remained virtually untapped for purposes of development, and were mostly deployed *rentier*-fashion in Great Britain. Net emigration approached 50 000 per annum, a level not far below the birthrate. It was the rising emigration above all that seemed to signal defeat. After more than a generation of self-government, it could no longer be presented as the evil fruit of British occupation, or invested with moving concepts of a folk-wandering, or with dreams of ultimate return. It sank to a mere issue of bread and butter, to the mundane and dispiriting truth that the new state was incapable of maintaining its existing population, let alone absorbing natural increase or calling back its exiles. Emigration was fast becoming the visible sign of failure—now of an interior failure in which the Irish people were wholly involved, and for which no outside scapegoat could be found.

Against this background, the First Economic Program of 1959 stands out as a daring if not desperate throw. 'In our present circumstances', the Program declared, 'we must be prepared to take risks under all headings—social, commercial and financial.' Starting with the Republic's financial stability and strength, on the one hand, and its miserable rate of growth on the other, it proposed to exploit the first in order to advance the second. The government enlarged the powers of the Central (or state) Bank and drove the commercial banks into supporting national expansion; channelled its own expenditure, so far as possible, into directly productive rather than socially useful undertakings; laid down a plan of development for private investment, especially in exports; and attempted to attract foreign capital and manufacturing techniques by 'tax holidays' and other forms of indirect subsidy, again especially favourable to export ventures.

Most of this was commonplace neo-Keynesianism, and the goal of the five-year plan, the doubling of the growth rate, was surely modest for it involved no more than a rise from 1 to 2 per cent. But if in many advanced economies such a program would have seemed unremarkable, in the Republic, with its century-old experience of contraction and decay, it was truly revolutionary. Aided by a fortunate upturn in world trade, its success astonished friend and foe. The growth rate in 1959–64 turned out to be 4 instead of 2 per cent, emigration dropped suddenly by two-thirds, and the population, which had fallen in an almost unbroken line from 6.5 million in 1841 to 2.8 million in 1961, had actually increased by 2.3 per cent by 1966. In few other western nations would these statistics have seemed especially encouraging, but in the Republic, so long steeped in economic defeat, they proclaimed a 'miracle'.

The change in political emphasis in and about 1959 proved lasting, all the more so as it was accompanied by general change of political generation. Lemass himself was almost the last survivor of the 1916–21 cohort in politics, and even he belonged in spirit to the new order: indeed, he was practically its midwife. The traditional staples of Irish politics—Civil War alignment, the meaning of sovereignty, the extent of jurisdiction, the nature of nationality, the language and native culture, and the rest—did not of course disappear; and some inevitably returned at times to the foreground in response to the northern crisis after 1969. But from 1958 onwards the essential issue was modernisation. Its most obvious form was that of wealth generation and the exploitation of the untapped resources inherent in the nation's physical situation, political soundness, bureaucratic ingenuity and educated people. Even while the First Economic Program was running its course, the foundations of a second were being laid. This struck down to deeper levels, and searched for more sophisticated and elaborate productive devices. The original 'Great Leap Forward' cast of mind was already dated. The object thereafter, and since, was to mesh progressively with a world economy.

Entry into the EEC at the beginning of 1973 was the apotheosis of this spirit and movement. Not merely did the net financial gains exceed even the original expectations— reaching over $A2 billion per annum in the 1990s—but also these provided for, among other things, the reorganisation and reinvigoration of Ireland's still-leading industry, agriculture, and the overhaul of much of the country's economic infrastructure. The usual extraordinarily high level of unemployment has persisted throughout the EC years, in part because of high birthrates in the immediate past. But this would surely have reached truly fearful proportions were it not for the greatly increased mobility of labour that the Common Market has induced. What part of western Europe will eventually be beyond the range of the commuter, and what will an Irish domicile ultimately mean?

Modernisation, however, is not to be considered only in material or quantitatively measurable terms. To a greater or less extent, depending on age, class, calling and location, the Republic has felt the impact of Europe—to say nothing of the traditional British pressures—in every aspect of its social life and values; and we are still, relatively speaking, only at the opening stage. At the same time, Ireland is uniquely placed to mediate the western European experience to the extra-European world. Such a capacity was apparent well before 1972, from the time of its entry into the United Nations in 1956, at least, and possibly, in shadowy form, even from the 1920s. In the very manner in which its nationhood was achieved, the new state was and is free from the taint and posthumous burdens of imperialism—at any rate of the more deadly sorts of imperialism, those of capital and power. On the contrary, it can claim much common ground with many other victims of the process.

The Irish Republic is a natural beneficiary of anti-British sentiment wherever it springs up in the world while yet a virtual ally of Great Britain on the leading domestic issue of the day, Northern Ireland. It is, by virtue of the American system of interest groups, the favoured friend of the United States while yet the historic exemplar of the African and Asian independence movements. Its international acceptability is such that, despite the tiny size of its military force, it has contributed heavily and repeatedly to peacekeeping work across the globe. It presents itself as almost pedantically neutral while appearing to be quite unneutrally efficient in humanitarian operations.

All this is ultimately the product of Irish history, which in certain senses Australia shares. At the same time, the Republic has been fortunate enough to have escaped, by and large, the charge of irredentism in its declared national objective of reabsorbing Northern Ireland. Such a charge would be internationally damaging in these Broad Church days. It has escaped, in part, because the objective has been modified without any need as yet to specify what modification would be acceptable, but mostly because the case can be presented as the final phase in the undoing of an old imperialism. Of course, in a world of simple graphic images and indigenous rights, it also helps to be a sea-girt island and to have been once a kingdom unto itself, however much the original succession to that kingdom may have been disputed or however long its crown may have rested on alien brows.

Affinities

In the history of Australia's relationship with Ireland, 1972 again presents itself as a date of considerable significance.

Specifically, it was then that the ALP, after nearly a quarter of a century in exile, returned to federal power. It was the overture to what was to become a protracted period of national Labor dominance, with seemingly effortless superiority in the end. This represents, if only in a strained and very limited sense, an Irish triumph. Despite the temporary incursions of the DLP, despite the broadening of the base of the Liberal Party and the effects of upward social mobility upon Catholics, and despite leaders such as Whitlam and Hawke who were thoroughly British in ancestry and political type, the Labor Party was in the 1980s, and still is, the 'natural' home of the Irish Catholic-derived of all classes below the affluent.

Although many other groups and interests had been drawn in to secure the ALP's power, the Catholic Irish had all the advantages of being a founding people in the party, with long-honed political skills and, often, distant political lineages and the most useful dynastic links. They formed a considerable proportion—probably well in excess of their due numbers—of the members, managers and leaders of the Federal and State Parliaments, and of the federal and local machines and satellites. They had become perhaps the largest single identifiable component in a politically dominant caste, even if they were bound by sentiment, personal network and common background rather than ideological positions. They were overdogs, or at least among the overdogs, at last.

It is a matter not only of office, authority, patronage or perquisites but also of cultural and social tone. The study of Irish-Australian identity, beginning with family derivations and chronicles, has grown exponentially in the past two decades. Fifty or even forty years ago, Australia and Ireland were virtually dead to one another so far as the mass of ordinary people—whether the descendants of emigrants or the descendants of those left behind—was concerned. The yearning for roots on the one hand and for outreach on the other, which began to be discernible worldwide in the revolutionary 1960s, has changed all that. Irish–Australian traffic, from the now bewildering interchange of heads of government and heads of state and politicians under innumerable banners to the inflow of singers, plays, musicians, instruments and writers of the new wave, has become so large and regular as to pass virtually unnoticed.

The twentieth-century historical affinities between Australia and the Irish Republic (as it now is) are surely ripe for exploration. Here are two countries whose political, governmental and other public forms and institutions derive very largely from a single source, Great Britain. In each case, context demanded that these be written out in a different idiom. In each case, moreover, formal constitutional autonomy had to be gradually developed into a deeper sort of psychological as well as an effectual independence. In each case, the new state was markedly exceptional in its own region, with corresponding conundrums of adjustment and corresponding opportunities to be seized. Of course, the differences between the two countries are deep and numerous. But the very fact that, in such contrasting fabrics, similar threads can be unpicked, and similar patterns can be so often glimpsed before the weave changes, makes the matching an exciting venture; and the shuttles that began their travelling in 1791 are still in movement.

References

1. Irish Parliamentary Debates, *Parliamentary Register*, ix, p. 129, 20 February 1789.
2. *Correspondence between the Right Honourable William Pitt and Charles Duke of Rutland, Lord Lieutenant of Ireland 1781–1787* (London, 1890), p.19.
3. R. Barry O'Brien, ed., *The Autobiography of Theobald Wolfe Tone*, 2 vols (Dublin, n.d.), I, p. 204.
4. Edith Mary Johnston, *Ireland in the Eighteenth Century* (Dublin, 1974), p. 174.
5. T. Wyse, *Historical Sketch of the Late Catholic Association of Ireland*, 2 vols (London, 1829), I, pp. 208–9.
6. Michael MacDonagh, *The Life of Daniel O'Connell* (London, 1903), p. 162.
7. David Kennedy, 'Education and the People' in *Social Life in Ireland 1800–45*, ed. R. B. McDowell (Dublin, 1957), pp. 60–4.
8. W.E.H. Lecky, *Leaders of Public Opinion in Ireland*, 2 vols (London, 1903), II, pp. 99–100.
9. W. L. Burn, 'Free Trade in Land: an Aspect of the Irish Question' in *Transactions of the Royal Historical Society*, 4th series, xxxi, p. 68.
10. Mark Finnane, *Police and Government: Histories of Policing in Australia* (Melbourne, 1994), p. 9.
11. J. O'Leary, *Recollections of Fenians and Fenianism*, 2 vols (London, 1896), I, p. 4.
12. W. J. O'Neill Daunt, Journal, 14 August 1859, quoted in R. F. Foster, *Modern Ireland 1600–1972* (London, 1988), p. 386.
13. O'Leary, op. cit., I, pp. 101–2.
14. Ibid, I, p. 27.

15. George Eliot, *Daniel Deronda* (Penguin Classics Edition, Harmondsworth, 1986), p. 875.
16. E. Curtis and R. B. McDowell, eds, *Irish Historical Documents* (London, 1943), pp. 311–13.
17. D. P. Moran, *The Philosophy of Irish Ireland* (Dublin, 1905), p. 48.
18. Curtis and McDowell, op. cit., p. 317–18.
19. T. P. Coogan, *Ireland Since the Rising* (London, 1966), p. 70.
20. Unpublished Home Office report on education, employment, local government and local elections in Northern Ireland (1938) quoted in David Harkness, *Northern Ireland since 1920* (Dublin, 1983), p. 80.
21. *N.I. House of Commons Debates*, xxvi, cols 1090–9 (24 April 1934).
22. Maurice Moynihan, ed., *Speeches and Statements by Eamon de Valera, 1917–73* (Dublin, 1980), p. 466.
23. *Ulster Year Book 1963–65* (Belfast, 1965), p. 265.
24. Harkness, op. cit., p. 164.
25. Harkness, ibid., p. 170.
26. John Whyte, 'Interpretations of the Northern Ireland Problems: An Appraisal', *Economic and Social Review*, ix, no. 4, p. 278.

Illustrative acknowledgments

xiii National Maritime Museum, Greenwich, A6406; **13** *Protestant Standard* 31/7/1869, National Library of Australia, NX 147; **80** *Illustrated Australian News* 6/9/1875 p.137, National Library of Australia; **91** *Illustrated London News* 10/7/1825, National Library of Australia, SF074.2ILL; **113** National Library of Australia, SR N080 PAM; **123** *Illustrated Sydney News* 21/2/1880, National Library of Australia; **139** Battye Library, 3728B/159; **154** *Smiths Weekly* 3/7/1920, National Library of Australia, NX 167; **184** *Irish Review* February 1954, National Library of Australia, NX 85.

Maps by Valda Brook.

Further reading

This brief list has been composed not so much for fellow professionals as to enable the general reader to pursue the main topics of the present book in more detail and depth, and sometimes to see them viewed from different angles.

F.S.L. Lyons, *Ireland Since the Famine* (London, 1971) is the most comprehensive and best-documented study of 1845–1969, the years from the Great Famine to the onset of the current 'Troubles' in Northern Ireland. An excellent general survey of even greater depth, covering most of the nineteenth century, is *A New History of Ireland* vol. V, edited by W.E. Vaughan (Oxford, 1989). This consists of lengthy essays by selected scholars on various aspects of the period; David Fitzpatrick's 'Emigration 1801–70' analyses the earlier Irish emigration to Australia as well as the broader issues involved in the massive outflow.

As works which give a longer and more complex perspective on the period I cover, J. C. Beckett, *The Making of Modern Ireland 1603–1923* (London, 1966), L. M. Cullen, *The Emergence of Modern Ireland, 1600–1900* (New York, 1981) and R. F. Foster, *Modern Ireland 1600–1972* (London, 1988), are warmly recommended.

For important interpretations of major historical, and particularly political–historical trends in modern Ireland, see Patrick O'Farrell, *Ireland's English Question* (Oxford, 1971), Oliver MacDonagh, *States of Mind: a Study of Anglo-Irish Conflict, 1780–1980* (London, 1983) and A.T.Q. Stewart, *The Narrow Ground: Aspects of Ulster, 1609–1969* (London, 1977).

Two series of short specialised books of a very high standard provide valuable insights and information for particular phases within the period 1790–1995. The relevant volumes in the Gill

History of Ireland are Edith Mary Johnston, *Ireland in the Eighteenth Century* (Dublin, 1974), Gearóid Ó Tuathaigh, *Ireland before the Famine* (Dublin, 1972), J. Lee, *The Modernisation of Irish Society 1848–1918* (Dublin, 1973), and John A. Murphy, *Ireland in the Twentieth Century* (Dublin, 1975), and in the Helicon History of Ireland, Donal McCartney, *The Dawning of Democracy: Ireland 1800–70* (Dublin, 1987), Pauric Travers, *Settlements and Divisions: Ireland 1870–1988* (Dublin, 1991) and David Harkness, *Northern Ireland since 1920* (Dublin, 1987).

Of the numerous studies of particular topics in years 1788–1995, three are selected for special mention because of their importance for fields stressed in the present book: S. J. Connolly, *Priests and People in Pre-Famine Ireland* (New York, 1982), K. Theodore Hopper, *Elections, Politics and Society in Ireland, 1832–85* (Oxford, 1984) and Samuel Clark, *Social Origins of the Irish Land War* (Princeton, 1979).

The main materials concerning recent major controversy over general interpretations of Irish history, both medieval and modern, may be most conveniently found in Ciaran Brady, ed., *Interpreting Irish History: the Debate on Historical Revisionism 1938–1994* (Dublin, 1994).

Volume VIII of *A New History of Ireland* (Oxford, 1982) edited by T. W. Moody, F. X. Martin and Francis Byrne, provides a very extensive chronology of Irish history, particularly of the modern period.

Index

208